D1081462

Withdrawn From Stock
Dublin City Public Libraries

Nadia Sawalha

Little Black Dress Diet

Nadia Sawalha is one of television's busiest presenters having never left our screens for the last 15 years. Nadia first came to fame as an actress playing Annie Palmer in *Eastenders* in the late 90s then switched to TV presenting as one of the original line-up of ITV's award-winning *Loose Women*. She then racked up credits including *City Hospital*, *Eating In The Sun*, *Passport To The Sun* and *Wanted Down Under* to name just a few. The popular mum-of-two won *Celebrity MasterChef*, and began her third career as one of the country's most in-demand TV cooks and food writers. She has written four cookbooks including the bestsellers *Stuffed Vine Leaves Saved My Life*, *Greedy Girl's Diet* and *Greedy Girl's Diet: Second Helpings!* Nadia also writes a weekly food column in the *Daily Mirror*. She co-presented 'The Real Woman's Little Black Dress Diet' on ITV's *Lorraine* and also has a regular cookery slot on the show. She recently hosted ITV's weekend cookery show *Saturday Cookbook*, and fronted the ITV show *Sunday Scoop* alongside Kaye Adams where she also cooked a sumptuous lunch for the guests each week. Nadia re-joined the panel of *Loose Women* in 2013 after a decade away and has since become a firm fixture on the show. In 2015 she made a return to acting with a role in ITV's multi-award-winning comedy *Benidorm*.

Nadia Sawalha

Little Black Dress Diet

Photography by
Maja Smend

Kyle Books

I would like to dedicate this book to my mum.
I love you Betty Boo x

First published in Great Britain in 2016 by
Kyle Books
an imprint of Kyle Cathie Limited
192–198 Vauxhall Bridge Road
London SW1V 1DX
general.enquiries@kylebooks.com
www.kylebooks.co.uk

10 9 8 7 6 5 4 3 2 1

ISBN: 978 0 85783 355 6

A CIP catalogue record for this title is available
from the British Library

Nadia Sawalha is hereby identified as the author
of this work in accordance with Section 77 of the
Copyright, Designs and Patents Act 1988.

NOTE: The nutritional information given with
each recipe is given per serving. The salt content
does not include seasoning salt as the amount you
add is discretionary. Serving suggestions are not
included in the analyses.

All rights reserved. No reproduction, copy or
transmission of this publication may be made
without written permission. No paragraph of
this publication may be reproduced, copied or
transmitted save with written permission or in
accordance with the provisions of the Copyright
Act 1956 (as amended). Any person who does any
unauthorised act in relation to this publication may
be liable to criminal prosecution and civil claims for
damages.

Text © Nadia Sawalha 2016
Food Photographs © Maja Smend 2016
Author Photographs © Nicky Johnston 2016
Illustrations © Aaron Blecha 2016
Design © Kyle Books 2016

Design: Nicky Collings
Photography: Maja Smend
Food styling: Lizzie Harris
Props styling: Rachel Jukes
Production: Nic Jones and Gemma John

Colour reproduction by F1 colour, London
Printed and bound in China by 1010 International
Printing Ltd.

Contents

Introduction

PEMBROKE BRANCH TEL. 6689575

Right, let's get this show on the road with my Little Black Dress Diet. It's time to get you ready to party! Little Black Dresses of the world, unite! I am here to finally make all your dreams come true. That's right. I'm going to help your dance partner find her mojo again. I'm going to revitalise that most vital of relationships between a girl and her Little Black Dress. Men don't understand the ways in which us women relate to our clothes. Yes, they may look at us and say 'you look nice', but for us the thought of looking good in a little black dress is about looking dynamite, feeling empowered, exuding confidence and not thinking for a minute about any blemishes. Well, let me show you the way back into your LBD!

But this time it's going to be different from any other diet!

I promise that on this diet you are going to eat an array of gorgeous, super-easy-to-prepare dishes that will tickle your taste buds as well as nourish your wonderful, powerful bodies. I also promise you that you will not go hungry because over the next 100 pages or so there is a wealth of wonderful, wholesome recipes for you to enjoy. Oh, and there's cake too! Yes, not only cake, but also fish and chips, burgers and wine, and many more usually 'forbidden foods'. I believe that if we cut out all of life's pleasures we can far too easily fall off the

wagon and end up bingeing our way back to a merry hell!

Imagine your Little Black Dress as a dance partner on the opposite side of the dance floor. Well, this diet is going to make your journey across that dance floor as enjoyable as the actual dance itself. This philosophy of enjoying what you eat while dieting is the way I lost and kept off three and a half stone. If it worked for me, it can work for you too and, believe me, throughout my life I've been on every diet known to man. I'd lose weight at the start, but in the end I would always put it all back on, plus a bit more too! But one day I decided enough was enough; I wanted to get off the misery merry-go-round. I wanted to be able to eat great food feeling guilt-free, but also be fit and healthy too.

What I didn't want to do was obsess about having the so-called 'perfect size eight' figure. It just wasn't right for my body type and chasing this fool's gold of a body for all those years had got me exactly nowhere.

I just wanted to look and feel as good as I could with my body type, not someone else's!

On this note, I'd like you to have a go at a little experiment I've carried out myself with great success. It's something I believe was a

Leabharlanna Poiblí Chathair Bhaile Átha Cliath
Dublin City Public Libraries

vital step on my road to finally getting the body I wanted. Ready? Right, go and find a hammer and a black bin liner (bear with me, I haven't lost my mind). OK, now go and get your bathroom scales (stay with me on this) because in a few moments we are going to do something with them that will literally change your life! You see, I'm convinced that our obsession in the West with jumping on and off the scales is responsible for so much of what I call our 'stinking thinking' about our bodies that so easily derails our best-laid plans. Let me set the scene…

You've had a great week on your 'diet'. You've been really 'good' – eating delicious, healthy food, exercising daily, not eating (too much) cake, drinking plenty of water, not

drinking (too much) alcohol and, hurrah, it's working! You feel the best you've felt in years! Your stomach feels flatter, your jeans are a tiny bit looser. You've got bags of energy and everyone has said they can 'really see a difference'. You are absolutely determined that you are going to keep this up until you are back into your favourite dress and beyond!

Then, brimming with hope and a tangible sense of achievement, you jump onto the scales for validation that you have indeed been 'good'. But, horror of all horrors, the dastardly dial swings to the right instead of the left! Not only have you not not lost any weight, but the scales are screaming that you've actually put on half a pound. Now this could be for any manner of reasons but it's too late. You've seen the dial and out of nowhere and at great speed the 'stinking thinking' crashes in and activates the self-destruct button in your head. All thoughts of how 'good' you've been disappear in a flash. Now you're 'bad'. You're so bad… you're so fat… you're so ugly… you're such a failure. You're depressed. Deflated. The image you saw in the mirror was just wishful thinking. And then a small gnawing feeling starts in your stomach. A pain, an ache, what is that?

Well, I know only too well what that is. It's your mind lying to you – telling you that you're hungry or maybe even starving. Telling you that you need to eat. You need to eat and push down how bloody miserable you're feeling. A biscuit. A bag of crisps. A sliver of cake. A slice of toast. Anything to stop feeling 'bad'. You open the fridge door... and the rest is history. It's a tragic cycle that so many women (and men) fall foul of just by stepping on their scales.

Well, no more girls!
No more slavery to the scales.

It's time to put them into that black bag and raise that hammer high above your head and smash the hell out of them. Go on, really give it to them! Smash, smash, smash!! Have a scream and shout too if you fancy it. Just let it all out. Now quietly and calmly gather yourself together and place the bag into the bin. And breathe. Ahhhhhhhhhhh. Your judge and jury have been trashed.

Now before you start worrying that I have lost my mind, let's just tap into how you felt as you smashed the living daylights out of those scales. If it's anything like the way I felt when I smashed up mine it will be a feeling of utter liberation. No more 'good girl/bad girl' nonsense. Just the will and determination to feel as fit and healthy as you can.

Ever since the day my scales got the shove, I've never again used them to tell me how I'm doing. I simply rely on the knowledge that I'm eating well and exercising enough. I also use my favourite little black dress to keep me on track. If the zip slips up without me breaking into a red-faced sweat, then I'm doing just fine. If not, then I just cut down a bit for a couple of days. So why not try the same tactic? It might just work for you too! Go on, dig out one of your favourite dresses

that no longer fits you the way you'd like it to and keep it on a hanger in full view as your inspiration. Then, every time you're tempted to eat something that will sabotage your plan or bunk off from your exercise class, just take a look at it. Close your eyes and really take yourself back to how great you felt when you were last wearing it. Because however you were before, you can be that again. Honestly, I know it sounds silly, but visualisation will be a very powerful tool in helping you to stay motivated over the next few months, so don't miss out!

I genuinely believe that when the scales don't reflect back what we feel or what our clothes are in fact suggesting (i.e. we are losing weight), we go into self-sabotage mode. I'm not just talking about eating loads or stuffing ourselves. I'm talking about a glass of wine when your resolve was stronger only minutes before you stepped on the scales. You don't walk to the shops, you drive. You decide to miss just one Pilates class. And then all these tiny micro 'give ups' build and build and, before you know it, you have an almighty uphill battle again.

So lose the vicious, snarling, inaccurate scales. How we look isn't just about what we weigh!

Are you feeling excited? The scales are no more. Your LBD is in full view now. All you need to do next is turn the page and get started because you deserve to look and feel the very best that you can for you!

Move that Body!

OK, I'm not going to pull any punches here. Ignoring this page is not an option. Thinking that you will just do the 'diet bit' and nothing else would be doing your health and weight-loss ambitions such a disservice that I'm afraid I'm going to have to harangue you into putting on those trainers and shifting your beautiful body every day! Yes, you heard me right. Every single day!

By simply exercising in some way (however small) every day, you will speed up your weight loss.

But of course weight loss won't be the only reward you will reap. You will also tone up and get some much-needed 'me time'. Now toning up and getting well-defined muscles is another reminder why smashing the scales will prove to be such a liberating act in your life. Muscle weighs more than fat. So to weigh something isn't necessarily to be overweight!

Most of us 'girls' spend a huge part of our lives looking after others: our kids, our fellas, our families and friends, and in my case two dogs and six guinea pigs (how did that happen?!) Now, of course, we wouldn't change that for the world, but unless we look after ourselves how on earth can we look after others? We need to lead by example. Studies prove that active mums have more active kids!

Now when I say I want you to exercise every day, it's important, of course, that you take it carefully at first if you haven't exercised for a while. The last thing we want is for you to injure yourself and end up on the sofa for weeks comforting yourself with family-sized bags of Doritos! I'm talking about bite-sized chunks of exercise to replace bite-sized chunks of chocolate. If you normally drive somewhere near to home, just once a week walk there. If you need something from upstairs, go up and down the stairs twice rather than just once. These things all add up.

When I first started exercising after years of sofa surfing and munching (food… not the sofa), I took it nice and slow and did nothing more than walk. I started with just ten minutes a day until I eventually got fit enough to run not one but two marathons. (Even when I see it written down I still can't believe it!) Although there will be no more marathons for me (my knees have made that quite clear) it doesn't mean I've given up on exercise. No way! In fact, I now love my exercise more than I ever did, and on pain of death no one is ever taking it away from me! (If you had asked me a few years ago if I ever would have said such a thing I would have laughed you out of the building!)

I really believe that the key to sticking to exercise is to do something you love.

Dance, play tennis, have wild sex twenty times a day, go to the gym; it really doesn't matter what you do as long as you actually do it. And these days it really doesn't have to cost you a penny either as you can learn almost anything on YouTube.

I have, finally, at the fabulous age of fifty-one, well and truly settled on my exercise passions of rebounding (more on that in a minute) and walking. In fact, I walk ten thousand steps or more (god, how I love my Fitbit) every day.

I think walking is the mothership of exercise as everyone has to do it anyway!

Walking really does so much more than simply get you from A to B too! It boosts weight loss, it's low impact (so good for those knees) and you don't need any special equipment or any pennies in your purse to do it. If anything, you'll save money. So get those walking shoes on and start to walk that fat away today! Surf the net for some great walking plans that will get you off the sofa and fit as a fiddle within weeks.

My other great exercise passion is rebounding and I bounce at least five times a week – just call me Tigger! Rebounding, put simply, is bouncing on a mini trampoline but not like you did as a kid where you would jump as high as you could. No. Rebounding is all about performing a series of small, controlled movements without ever jumping higher than 15cm. It really can be done by everyone too. Young, old, sick, frail – anyone can rebound, and I love exercise where there can be no excuses. I also love anything I can do in front of the telly!

Rebounding has zero impact, has a high-calorie burn (so brings on weight loss), and improves muscle tone and bone strength. In fact, the list of health benefits goes on and on – but you don't have to take my word for it. Just google rebounding and you will see exactly why I'm so passionate about it. It was even described in a NASA study 'as the most efficient, effective form of exercise yet devised by man', so put that in your pipe and smoke it! But the point is, I have found my mojo and I urge you with every fibre of my being to search until you find yours. It really is the key to a happy, healthy life. Well that and the occasional cake!

Three-Week Plan

I've devised this stricter three-week plan for those of you who want to move things a bit quicker. I've taken out extra indulgences like desserts and alcohol that are in the six-week plan. I do NOT recommend this in the long-term, as I find if we go too long without our indulgences, it only leads to the dreaded binge! You can, of course, add the odd small glass of wine here and there, and the odd dessert, but your weight loss will be quicker if you don't. If you are suffering with real hunger pangs, you can always have a bowl of Magic Weight-loss Soup (page 56) and you can add as much green veg as you like to any of the dishes. Make sure you drink plenty of water, and green tea gives the metabolism a boost too. You can drink diet drinks (better for the bod if you don't, though), as well as tea and coffee.

Week 1	Breakfast	Lunch	Dinner
MONDAY	Skinny Bitch Juice (page 34)	Waldorf Salad Jackets (page 82)	Chicken + Noodles (page 94)
TUESDAY	If You Can't Beet 'em Juice (page 34)	Salmon Penne Pasta Salad (page 76)	Chicken in Black Bean Sauce (page 99)
WEDNESDAY	Poached Eggs + Avocado (page 22)	Asian Lettuce Wraps (page 66)	Baked Mackerel, Fennel + Tomatoes (page 118)
THURSDAY	Power Smoothie (page 25). Add 6–8 almonds.	Courgetti Puttanesca (page 73)	Turkey Meatloaf (page 128)
FRIDAY	Boiled Egg + Beans (page 28)	Chicken + Avocado Wraps (page 63)	Tomato + Avocado Courgetti or Teriyaki Chicken (pages 122–123)
SATURDAY	Breakfast in a Roll (page 36)	Mushroom Soup (page 54)	Cumin + Coriander Lamb (page 125)
SUNDAY	Amazing American Banana Bread (page 30)	Egg Jumble (page 89)	Salmon + Asparagus en Papillote (page 130)

Week 2	Breakfast	Lunch	Dinner
MONDAY	If You Can't Beet 'em Juice (page 34)	Courgetti Puttanesca (page 73)	Chicken Tickle Tikka (page 93)
TUESDAY	Funky Frittatas (page 33)	Beautiful BLT (page 60)	Sesame Beef + Cucumber Noodles (page 113)
WEDNESDAY	Super Low-calorie Brekkie (page 28)	Waldorf Salad Jackets (page 82)	Pork Souvlaki (page 103)
THURSDAY	Breakfast in a Roll (page 36)	Shirley Valentine Salad (page 83)	Lean Lasagne (pages 105–106)
FRIDAY	Buongiorno Sandwich (page 44)	Magic Weight-loss Soup and Courgette Fritters (pages 56 and 88)	Bistro-style Mussels (page 117)
SATURDAY	Boiled Egg + Beans (page 28)	Celery, Carrot + Hummus Wraps (page 64)	Bream in a Parcel (page 127)
SUNDAY	Quinoa Porridge (page 38)	Beetroot + Horseradish Soup (page 52)	Teriyaki Chicken (page 123)

Week 3	Breakfast	Lunch	Dinner
MONDAY	Cheesy Spinach Omelette (page 29)	Nutty Fish Salad (page 68)	Chicken 'Bruschettas' (page 100)
TUESDAY	Skinny Bitch Juice (page 34)	Five-star Turkey Club Sandwich (page 70)	Celeriac Cottage Pie (page 129)
WEDNESDAY	Poached Eggs + Avocado (page 22)	Chicken Noodle Soup (page 59)	Pork Souvlaki (page 103)
THURSDAY	Power Smoothie (page 25)	Cheese + Onion Sandwich (page 65)	Cumin + Coriander Lamb (page 125)
FRIDAY	Breakfast in a Roll (page 36)	Parsnip + Apple Soup (page 57)	Burgers + Sweet Potato Fries (page 108)
SATURDAY	Funky Frittatas (page 33)	Asian Lettuce Wraps (page 66)	Veggie Curry in a Hurry (page 120)
SUNDAY	Amazing American Banana Bread (page 30)	Cauliflower Power Pizza (page 74)	Roasted Garlic Chicken with Roast Jacket Potatoes and green veg (pages 97 and 98)

Six-Week Plan

This sensational six-week plan certainly allows for more indulgences than the three-week one. So the weight loss will be a wee bit slower but it's not quite so challenging as the three-week plan. You will get to eat all the slightly higher-calorie dishes from the book as well as a little extra rice, potatoes or pasta alongside your evening meal. You'll also get to enjoy dessert a couple of times a week – and guess what else? A full roast dinner and the odd glass of wine are on the menu at weekends too! So, even though you'll be able to eat lots of gorgeous food, if you stick to the plan and exercise almost every day, you will (I promise) take the weight off and keep it off. So let the journey begin, girls!

Week 1	Breakfast	Lunch	Dinner
MONDAY	Cheesy Spinach Omelette (page 29)	Parsnip + Apple Soup (page 57). Add cheese on toast, using one slice of wholemeal bread and a matchbox-sized piece of cheese.	Chicken Tickle Tikka (page 93). Add 2 tablespoons of brown rice per person.
TUESDAY	Quinoa Porridge (page 38)	Salmon Penne Pasta Salad (page 76)	Burgers + Sweet Potato Fries Skinny Soft Ice Cream (pages 108 and 153)
WEDNESDAY	Smoked Salmon + Cream Cheese Bagel (page 26)	Mushroom Soup (page 54)	Cabbage Rolls with Pork + Rice (pages 110–111)
THURSDAY	Poached Eggs + Avocado (page 22)	Nutty Fish Salad (page 68)	Lean Lasagne and Satsumas Dipped in Dark Chocolate (pages 105 and 139)
FRIDAY	Amazing American Banana Bread (page 30)	Shirley Valentine Salad (page 83)	Fish + Chips (page 114)
SATURDAY	Buongiorno Sandwich (page 44)	Chilli Beef with Vanilla + Pear Custard Tarts (pages 85 and 140)	Chicken in Black Bean Sauce (page 99). Add 150g packaged rice noodles for 4 people. 6-week treat: small glass of wine.
SUNDAY	Bacon Butty (page 37)	Asian Lettuce Wraps (page 66). Stir 2 tablespoons of rice per person into the beef.	Roasted Garlic Chicken, Roast Jacket Potatoes and Saintly Sage + Onion Balls and Apple Pies with Heart (pages 97, 98 and 154).

Week 2	Breakfast	Lunch	Dinner
MONDAY	Power Smoothie (page 25) Add 6–8 almonds.	Beautiful BLT (page 60)	Chicken 'Bruschettas' (page 100)
TUESDAY	Fry-up in a pan (page 46)	Beetroot + Horseradish Soup (page 52). Add two small slices of bread and a scraping of butter.	Sesame Beef & Cucumber Noodles (page 113) Date + Apricot Balls (page 152)
WEDNESDAY	Skinny Bitch Juice (page 34)	Waldorf Salad Jackets (page 82)	Baked Mackerel, Fennel +Tomatoes (page 118)
THURSDAY	Sausage + Egg Muffin (page 42)	Lemon Pepper Tuna Sandwich (page 71)	Veggie Curry in a Hurry. Add 4 tablespoons of rice per person. Skinny Soft Ice Cream (pages 120 and 153).
FRIDAY	Amazing American Banana Bread (page 30)	Courgette Fritters (page 88) served with a mixed salad and a dressing of 1 teaspoon of vinegar, 1 teaspoon mustard and ½ tablespoon olive oil	Turkey Meatloaf (page 128)
SATURDAY	Watermelon, Feta + Tomato Salad (page 49)	Five-star Turkey Club Sandwich (page 70)	Cumin + Coriander Lamb (page 125) and Blueberry Mug Cake (page 143)
SUNDAY	Eggs en Cocotte (page 41)	Cheese + Onion Sandwich (page 65)	Chicken + Noodles (page 94) and Homemade Fruit Jellies (page 144)

Six-Week Plan
continued

Week 3	Breakfast	Lunch	Dinner
MONDAY	Cheesy Spinach Omelette (page 29)	Grilled Mushroom Burgers (page 81)	Teriyaki Chicken (page 123)
TUESDAY	Bacon Butty (page 37)	Magic Weight-loss Soup (page 56)	Pork Souvlaki (page 103). Satsumas Dipped in Dark Chocolate (page 139)
WEDNESDAY	Buongiorno Sandwich (page 44)	Baked Sea Bass with Tomato Pesto Salad (page 78)	Mexican Rice (page 132) and small glass of red wine.
THURSDAY	Boiled Egg + Beans (page 28). You could swap the beans for one slice of toast cut into soldiers.	Chicken + Avocado Wraps (page 63)	Burgers + Sweet Potato Fries (page 108) and Vanilla + Pear Custard Tarts (page 140).
FRIDAY	Breakfast in a Roll (page 36)	Celery, Carrot + Hummus Wraps (page 64). Add a serving of any of the lunchtime soups.	Bream in a Parcel (page 126). Add Sweet Potato Chips (see Fish + Chips recipe page 114).
SATURDAY	Amazing American Banana Bread (page 30)	Cauliflower Power Pizza (page 74)	Celeriac Cottage Pie (page 129)
SUNDAY	Funky Frittatas (page 33)	Veggie Coconut Soup (page 86)	Salmon Asparagus en Papillotte (page 130) with Greedy Girl's Chocolate Pudding (page 149).

Week 4	Breakfast	Lunch	Dinner
MONDAY	If You Can't Beet 'em Juice (page 34)	Courgetti Puttanesca (page 73)	Lamb's Liver Arabic-style (page 134). Add 2 tablespoons of rice per person.
TUESDAY	Quinoa Porridge (page 38)	Salmon Penne Pasta Salad (page 76)	Sesame Beef + Cucumber Noodles with Skinny Soft Ice Cream (pages 113 and 153)
WEDNESDAY	Smoked Salmon + Cream Cheese Bagel (page 26)	Chicken Noodle Soup (page 59)	Cabbage Rolls with Pork + Rice (page 110)
THURSDAY	Poached Eggs + Avocado (page 22)	Nutty Fish Salad (page 68)	Chicken + Noodles (page 94) and Satsumas Dipped in Dark Chocolate (page 139).
FRIDAY	Morning-after Smoothie (page 48)	Shirley Valentine Salad (page 83)	Turkey Meatloaf (page 128)
SATURDAY	Buongiorno Sandwich (page 44)	Greedy Girls Love Carbs Pasta Salad (page 77) and Vanilla + Pear Custard Tarts (page 140).	Chicken in Black Bean Sauce (page 99). Add 150g packaged rice noodles for 4 people. 6-week treat: small glass of wine.
SUNDAY	Bacon Butty (page 37)	Asian Lettuce Wraps (page 66). Stir 2 tablespoons of rice per person into the beef.	Roasted Garlic Chicken, Roast Jacket Potatoes and Saintly Sage + Onion Balls and Apple Pies with Heart (pages 97, 98 and 154).

Six-Week Plan continued

Week 5	Breakfast	Lunch	Dinner
MONDAY	Cheesy Spinach Omelette (page 29)	Waldorf Salad Jackets (page 82)	Burgers + Sweet Potato Fries (page 108)
TUESDAY	Skinny Bitch Juice (page 34)	Egg Jumble (page 89)	Pork Souvlaki (page 103) Satsumas Dipped in Dark Chocolate (page 139)
WEDNESDAY	Super-low Calorie Brekkie (page 28)	Baked Sea Bass with Tomato Pesto Salad (page 78)	Bistro-style Mussels (page 117)
THURSDAY	Boiled Egg + Beans (page 28). You could swap the beans for one slice of toast cut into soldiers.	Veggie Coconut Soup (page 86)	Veggie Curry in a Hurry (page 120). Add 2 tablespoons of rice per person. Vanilla + Pear Custard Tarts (page 140)
FRIDAY	Breakfast in a Roll (page 36)	Magic Weight-loss Soup (page 56)	Bream in a Parcel (page 127). Add Sweet Potato Chips (see Fish + Chips recipe page 114).
SATURDAY	Watermelon, Feta + Tomato Salad (page 49)	Cauliflower Power Pizza (page 74)	Teriyaki Chicken (page 123) 6 week treat: small glass of wine
SUNDAY	Funky Frittatas (page 33)	Mushroom Soup (page 54)	Tomato + Avocado Courgetti. Apple Pies with Heart (pages 122 and 154)

Week 6	Breakfast	Lunch	Dinner
MONDAY	Power Smoothie (page 25) Add 6–8 almonds.	Beautiful BLT (page 60)	Chicken 'Bruschettas' (page 100)
TUESDAY	Sausage + Egg Muffin (pages 42–43)	Beetroot + Horseradish Soup (page 52). Add two small slices bread and a scraping of butter.	Pork Souvlaki (page 103) with Date + Apricot Balls (page 152)
WEDNESDAY	If You Can't Beet 'em Juice (page 34)	Waldorf Salad Jackets (page 82)	Baked Mackerel, Fennel + Tomatoes (page 118)
THURSDAY	Quinoa Porridge (page 38)	Lemon Pepper Tuna Sandwich (page 71)	Veggie Curry in a Hurry (page 120). Add 4 tablespoons of rice per person with Skinny Soft Ice Cream (page 153).
FRIDAY	Buongiorno Sandwich (page 44)	Courgette Fritters (page 88) served with a mixed salad and a dressing of 1 teaspoon vinegar, 1 teaspoon mustard and ½ tablespoon olive oil	Turkey Meatloaf (page 128)
SATURDAY	Fry-up in a Pan (page 46)	Courgetti Puttanesca (page 73)	Cumin + Coriander Lamb with Mini Victoria Sandwiches (pages 125, 150)
SUNDAY	Eggs en Cocotte (page 41)	Cheese + Onion Sandwich (page 65)	Roasted Garlic Chicken, Roast Jacket Potatoes and Saintly Sage + Onion Balls. Homemade Fruit Jellies (pages 97, 98 and 144)

Breakfast

Poached Eggs + Avocado

Trust me on this: you won't miss fattening bacon with this lovely breakfast of avocado and eggs full of good fats and muscle-building protein. Listen to me, Miss Goody Two-Shoes!

194 Calories | 11.1g Fat | 2.7g Saturates | 1.6g Sugars | 1.1g Salt

SERVES 4

a small dash of vinegar

4 eggs

4 small slices of rye, wholemeal
   or granary bread, toasted

1 small avocado, peeled and
   sliced

$1/2$ teaspoon chilli flakes

24–32 cherry tomatoes, halved

sea salt and freshly ground
   black pepper

When poaching eggs, it is really important to make sure they are fresh.

Heat a pan of water until it is steadily simmering, then add the vinegar – you should see tiny little bubbles. Now crack each egg into a separate cup. Then, using a spoon or a whisk, create a gentle whirlpool in the water and slowly tip each egg into the water. Cook for 3–5 minutes, depending on how soft you like them.

Remove the eggs with a slotted spoon and, very importantly, drain on kitchen paper. (Soggy poached eggs? No thanks!)

Serve on your chosen toasted bread with the sliced avocado. Finish with a sprinkling of sea salt, a twist of black pepper and a flourish of chilli flakes. Serve with the cherry tomatoes alongside.

Power Smoothie

Ahhhh...the simple joy of bunging handfuls of delicious, nourishing ingredients into a blender and making something even more delicious! This smoothie is packed full of nutrients so can power you through your day.

96 Calories | 2.6g Fat | 0.4g Saturates | 11g Sugars | 0.1g Salt

SERVES 2

1 small banana

8–10 raspberries

8–10 blueberries

½ teaspoon of vanilla extract
   (optional)

300ml almond, soya
   or skimmed milk

Put all the ingredients in a blender and blitz until smooth. Serve with ice and enjoy.

Tip

Don't overdo it on the fruit. Limit yourself to only two pieces a day as they contain surprisingly high amounts of natural sugars.

Smoked Salmon +
Cream Cheese Bagel

Eating one of these makes me feel like I'm in New York and I luuuuurve New York! I also love whoever invented the super-thin bagel because it means I can still enjoy a taste of New York without feeling too much carb guilt!

256 Calories | 5g Fat | 1.5g Saturates | 5.3g Sugars | 3.2g Salt

SERVES 1

1 super-thin bagel (isn't it great, they sell these in all supermarkets)

1 tablespoon low-fat cream cheese

1 slice smoked salmon (big enough to cover bagel)

3 slices of red onion

1 teaspoon capers, drained

juice of ¼ lemon

freshly ground black pepper

Lightly toast the bagel, spread with the cream cheese, then load in the smoked salmon, red onion and finally the capers. Finish with a squeeze of lemon juice and a good grinding of black pepper.

Tip

Make time for a bit of exercise every day, even if it's just a 20-minute walk!

Boiled Egg + Beans

I've made this breakfast for one because only those determined to get into their little black dress would swap buttery toast for green beans!

94 Calories | 5.9g Fat | 1.6g Saturates | 1.3g Sugars | 0.2g Salt

SERVES 1

1 egg

10 green beans (or asparagus when in season)

sea salt and freshly ground black pepper

Heat a pan of water until it reaches boiling point, then put in the egg, reduce the heat and simmer for 3 minutes. I usually steam my green beans over the egg as it simmers, as steaming retains all the vitamins.

Serve the egg in an egg cup with the beans alongside for dipping. Season with a little salt and some freshly ground black pepper.

Super Low-calorie Brekkie

If you were hoping to fast this morning but just couldn't bring yourself to do it, have this super low-calorie breakfast instead.

66 Calories | 0.4g Fat | 0.1g Saturates | 11.2g Sugars | 0.1g Salt

SERVES 1

1 kiwi, peeled and roughly chopped

3 tablespoons fat-free yogurt

1 tablespoon blueberries

1/4 teaspoon vanilla extract

Simply mix together all the ingredients and eat slowly with a teaspoon so it lasts longer.

Cheesy Spinach Omelette

This is a cutie of a breakfast because if you don't want to break your fast in the morning it makes a great lunch too! I've taken the yolks out of this recipe to reduce the calorie count but feel free to keep them in if you want.

158 Calories | 5.7g Fat | 1.7g Saturates | 2.2g Sugars | 1g Salt

SERVES 1

1 teaspoon olive oil

2 egg whites

2 teaspoons grated Parmesan

a handful of spinach,
    coarsely chopped

1 slice of rye bread, toasted

tomatoes, to taste

basil (optional)

freshly ground black pepper

Heat a non-stick frying pan and pour in the olive oil. Spread it around the pan with a pastry brush.

While the pan gets nice and hot, whisk the egg whites with a little black pepper. Pour the egg mixture into the pan and then sprinkle the Parmesan over the top. Add the spinach and, using a rubber spatula, gently fold the omelette over and then remove the pan from the heat.

Serve on the toasted rye bread with the tomatoes and, if you have some basil lying around, that would also be rather nice on top.

Amazing American Banana Bread

I cannot claim the credit for this recipe as I stole it from my auntie when I was staying with her in Los Angeles last year. I know, how evil am I?! But I did it for all you girls trying to get into that little black dress!

226 Calories | 3.2g Fat | 0.4g Saturates | 22.8g Sugars | 0.2g Salt

MAKES 16 SLICES/

SERVES 8

3 large very ripe bananas,
   peeled

100g soft brown sugar

3 egg whites

1/2 tablespoon coconut,
   olive or sunflower oil

70g fat-free Greek yogurt

60ml apple juice

110g plain flour

100g wholemeal flour

1 teaspoon baking powder

1 tablespoon each of pumpkin
   seeds and sunflower seeds

honey or maple syrup, to serve
   (optional)

Preheat the oven to 180°C/gas mark 4. Grease and line a loaf tin with baking paper. Mash the bananas in a large bowl with the sugar. Then mix in the egg whites and oil. Stir in the yogurt and apple juice, then the plain and wholemeal flours and baking powder. Pour into the prepared loaf tin, sprinkle with the seeds and bake for 50 minutes–1 hour until well-risen and golden.

Remove from the oven and leave to cool for 10–15 minutes in the tin. Then remove and cool on a wire rack. Eat either as it is or toast and serve with a little honey or maple syrup.

Funky Frittatas

This dish has it all: great looks and a personality to match! This is a fantastic way to start your day as it's packed full of protein and five of your seven-a-day.

168 Calories | 11g Fat | 3g Saturates | 3g Sugars | 0.6g Salt

SERVES 6

olive oil, for greasing

6 large eggs

1 carrot, peeled and coarsely grated

1 courgette, coarsely grated

a handful of fresh flat-leaf parsley, chopped

$1/4$ onion, grated or finely chopped

$1/2$ red pepper, finely chopped

2 tablespoons peas

6 slices of tomato

sea salt and freshly ground black pepper

Preheat the oven to 190°C/gas mark 5. Very lightly grease a six-hole non-stick muffin tray with olive oil.

Whisk the eggs in a large bowl with a good pinch of salt and black pepper. Add the carrot and courgette. Then stir in the remaining ingredients, except the tomato, and pour into the muffin tray. Top each muffin with a slice of tomato. Bake for 25 minutes, or until just set.

Skinny Bitch Juice

Some may shoot me down for this claim, but this juice leaves me feeling skinny, as its diuretic quality can shift buckets of fluid! So, come on, sue me!

77 Calories | 1.5g Fat | 0.1g Saturates | 6.2g Sugars | 0g Salt

SERVES 1

6–8 celery sticks

1 whole cucumber

2.5cm piece of fresh ginger, peeled

$\frac{1}{2}$ bunch of fresh flat-leaf parsley

a large handful of spinach

Put all the ingredients through a juicer. Serve over ice.

If You Can't Beet 'em Juice

As the beetroot is sweet I use a cooking apple here.

131 Calories | 0.9g Fat | 0.2g Saturates | 21.4g Sugars | 3.3g Salt

SERVES 1

2 medium raw beetroots, peeled

1 cooking apple, peeled, cored and sliced

3 carrots, roughly chopped

1.25cm piece of fresh ginger, peeled (optional)

juice of 1 small lemon

Put all the ingredients through a juicer. Serve over ice.

Breakfast in a Roll

Fancy a really nice breakfast and no washing-up whatsoever? I once made 20 of these when I had a big house party – one baking tray equalled 20 people fed! But for now, let's make do with one each.

195 Calories | 7.5g Fat | 2.1g Saturates | 1.1g Sugars | 1.5g Salt

SERVES 4

4 soft or crusty bread rolls

4 small slices of ham

4 eggs, at room temperature

1 tablespoon finely chopped
fresh flat-leaf parsley

Preheat the oven to 180°C/gas mark 4. Cut the tops off the rolls and then, using a sharp knife, cut a circle and scoop out the centres (I make them into breadcrumbs and pop them in the freezer).

Now line the bread roll 'bowl' with a slice of ham. If possible, use a whole piece otherwise the egg will seep through the crack into the bread. Now break an egg into each bread bowl. Put the top back on each roll. Wrap with foil and bake for 10–15 minutes.

Have a look after 10 minutes and see if you want to leave it a bit longer. If you like your eggs hard, they will probably take about 20 minutes. Sprinkle with the parsley before serving.

Bacon Butty

Sometimes only a bacon butty will do when you have the hangover from hell. Consume with water!

291 Calories | 13.9g Fat | 6g Saturates | 2.1g Sugars | 2.8g Salt

SERVES 1

2 slices of back bacon

2 slices of wholemeal bread

a little butter or tomato ketchup

1 tomato, sliced

Grill the bacon until it's the way you like it – crispy for me, please! Then remove the fat with a knife. Toast the bread and very lightly butter it or spread with ketchup. Then load in the bacon and tomato and top with the other slice of bread.

Tip

Cut down on your carbs – cut the tops off your rolls and then, using a sharp knife, cut a circle and scoop out the centres!

Quinoa Porridge

I hate porridge but I like this one made with quinoa, the god of superfoods, as it's a complete protein – a great alternative to more starchy grains. You can also make it with oats or millet instead.

243 Calories | 2.6g Fat | 0.5g Saturates | 22.2g Sugars | 0.3g Salt

SERVES 2

80g quinoa

400ml skimmed, almond,
   rice or light coconut milk

1 apple, grated

1 tablespoon top-quality
   maple syrup or honey

1 teaspoon vanilla extract

100g raspberries, blueberries or
   grapes, halved

Put the quinoa in a sieve and rinse under cold running water. Put it in a non-stick pan with 350ml of the milk, the apple and maple syrup or honey. Bring to the boil, then reduce the heat and simmer for 10 minutes.

Stir in the remaining milk and the vanilla extract, and cook for a further 3–4 minutes. Taste, and if you think it needs more sweetener, add a little more syrup, but try to bear it without – you will get used to it. Top with the raspberries, blueberries or grapes.

Eggs
en Cocotte

Eggs on what?? Ha ha ha! Eggs are a great choice
for breakfast as the protein keeps you
fuller for longer so you're less likely to reach for
a mid-morning biscuit.

239 Calories | 12g Fat | 3g Saturates | 1.3g Sugars | 2.4g Salt

SERVES 4

1 tablespoon olive oil

4 slices of lean smoked ham,
  chopped

1 tomato, finely chopped

1 teaspoon dried oregano

4 large eggs

4 small slices of rye or
  wholemeal bread, toasted

sea salt and freshly ground
  black pepper

Preheat the oven to190°C/gas mark 5. Using a pastry brush,
coat the inside of four 8.5cm ramekins with the oil. Into
each ramekin, drop in the ham, then the tomato, a sprinkle
of oregano and finally crack in the egg. Season with salt and
black pepper.

Now put the ramekins into a roasting tray and pour boiling
water into the tray about one quarter of the way up the side
of the ramekins. Bake for 12–15 minutes for runny yolks,
15–18 minutes for soft-cooked yolks or 20 minutes for hard-
cooked yolks.

When they're done, eat immediately with toast soldiers (no
more than one small slice each).

Sausage + Egg Muffin

Not naughty & still nice!

I found inspiration for this recipe on an American website, and it is so close to an actual McDonald's, but healthy! I suggest you make a whole trayful of these pick-me-ups and keep them in the freezer for hangover emergencies. And when I say American cheese I mean that orange plastic-y stuff!

300 Calories | 12.9g Fat | 4.3g Saturates | 2.4g Sugars | 2.1g Salt

SERVES 12

low-calorie cooking spray

12 large eggs

12 low-fat sausages

12 x 100 per cent wholemeal
   muffins

12 slices of low-calorie
   American cheese

freshly ground black pepper

Preheat the oven to 180°C/gas mark 4. Grease two six-hole muffin trays with low-calorie cooking spray. Break an egg to each hole and with a fork gently break the yolk (so the baked egg will be flat). Sprinkle with black pepper and bake for 10–20 minutes, or until set and completely cooked. (The time will vary depending on the type of muffin tray you are using, so keep a close watch.)

While the eggs are baking, preheat the grill to moderate. Slit the sausages open, remove the skin and reform the sausage meat into 12 patties. Grill the patties for a couple of minutes on each side.

When the eggs and sausages are cooked, split open the muffins. Stack a slice of cheese (I fold it so it doesn't hang over the side), a sausage patty and a baked egg, then top with the other half muffin.

Tip

Add lemon juice to warm water for your morning wake-up remedy – it'll help kick start your metabolism, rehydrate your body and set you up for an energetic day ahead!

To freeze and reheat in the microwave, wrap each muffin in baking paper, place in a freezer bag or box and freeze. To reheat from frozen, leave the muffin in the paper and heat for about 3 minutes at half-power, turning halfway through. If thawed, heat for 40–60 seconds at full power.

To freeze and reheat in the oven, wrap each muffin in foil, place in a freezer bag and freeze. Preheat the oven to 180°C/gas mark 4. Place the muffin on a baking sheet and reheat for 15–20 minutes if thawed, 30–40 minutes if frozen.

Buongiorno Sandwich

This breakfast takes me back to my honeymoon on the Amalfi Coast – and every time I make it, it's like flying the Italian flag for the first time.

294 Calories | 5.4g Fat | 0.5g Saturates | 2.9g Sugars | 1.9g Salt

SERVES 1

100g ciabatta bread,
   sliced in half

6 cherry tomatoes on the vine,
   sliced

1 teaspoon olive oil

3 fresh basil leaves,
   chopped

sea salt and freshly ground
   black pepper

Lightly toast the ciabatta, then squish the tomatoes onto the bread and drizzle with the oil before sprinkling the salt and black pepper on top. Finish with a flourish of basil.

Tip

A doughnut, although bloody lovely, doesn't give you much energy!

Fry-up
in a Pan

If you're feeling delicate you'll like this idea of
bunging your fry-up in one pan. You can crash on
the sofa while it's cooking in the oven…

216 Calories | 8.9g Fat | 2g Saturates | 1.4g Sugars | 0.7g Salt

SERVES 4

500g potatoes, diced

1 tablespoon olive oil

16 cherry tomatoes

200g button mushrooms

4 eggs

sea salt and freshly ground
   black pepper

Preheat the oven to 200°C/gas mark 6. Put the potatoes in
a large non-stick, ovenproof pan or roasting tin, drizzle with
the oil and season to taste. Bake for 30 minutes. Then add the
tomatoes and mushrooms and bake for a further 20 minutes,
or until the potatoes are tender.

Remove from the oven, make four holes and crack an egg into
each one. Return to the oven for 3–8 minutes, depending on
how you like your eggs.

Morning-after Smoothie

Have you got earplugs… you might just need them for the blitz bit of this.

94 Calories | 0.5g Fat | 0.1g Saturates | 14g Sugars | 0.2g Salt

SERVES 1

a large handful of spinach

1cm piece of fresh ginger, peeled

200ml coconut water

a handful of frozen mixed berries

1 teaspoon honey

Put all the ingredients through a juicer.

Serve over ice.

Watermelon, Feta + Tomato Salad

Now I know you are thinking 'She's put this in the wrong section'. Yes, it's a salad in the Breakfast chapter but this is one of my favourite breakfasts, especially if the sun is out.

86 Calories | 4.4g Fat | 1.4g Saturates | 4.9g Sugars | 0.1g Salt

SERVES 4

1 tablespoon olive oil

2 tablespoons white wine,
    balsamic or raspberry vinegar

10 cherry tomatoes

1 whole, preferably organic,
    cucumber, cut into cubes

200g watermelon, cubed

100g light feta cheese, cubed

1 tablespoon finely chopped
    fresh mint, to garnish

1 tablespoon finely chopped
    fresh basil, to garnish

sea salt and freshly ground
    black pepper

To make the dressing, whisk the oil and vinegar in a small bowl. Put the remaining ingredients, except the mint and basil, in a pretty serving dish and drizzle the dressing over the top. Serve with the mint and basil scattered over the top.

Tip

It really pays off to decide what you are going to have for breakfast the night before. It feels great to get up with a plan already in place.

Lunch

Beetroot + Horseradish Soup

I absolutely love horseradish and beetroot, hence this gorgeous soup! I hope you'll love it as much as I do, because it's not only delicious but also super good for you, which means if you have it for lunch you've got hours to feel smug before bed.

160 Calories | 3.2g Fat | 0.4g Saturates | 15.9g Sugars | 0.8g Salt

SERVES 4–6

1 tablespoon olive oil

1 large onion, chopped

250g sweet potatoes,
   peeled and chopped

850g raw beetroot,
   peeled and chopped

600ml hot chicken or
   vegetable stock

4 tablespoons horseradish sauce

freshly ground black pepper

Heat the oil in a large pan and cook the onion for 4–6 minutes until softened and translucent but not coloured. Then add the potatoes and beetroot. Fry for 3–4 minutes, stirring constantly. Now pour in the stock and bring to the boil. Reduce the heat and simmer for about 25 minutes, or until the vegetables are tender.

Transfer to a blender, add the horseradish sauce and blitz until smooth. Gently reheat and serve garnished with black pepper.

Mushroom Soup

I can never quite believe it, but even my kids eat this and I have the fussiest kids in the world! So I usually make a double batch and keep it in the freezer for those can't-be-bothered days.

136 Calories | 2.8g Fat | 0.4g Saturates | 5.5g Sugars | 1.8g Salt

SERVES 4

$^{1}/_{2}$ tablespoon olive oil

1 large onion, chopped

2 garlic cloves, chopped

1 potato the size of your palm, peeled and diced

700g of your favourite mushrooms, sliced

600ml chicken or vegetable stock

2–3 sprigs of fresh thyme

1 bay leaf

100g fat-free crème fraîche

sea salt and freshly ground black pepper

Heat the oil in a saucepan and fry the onion and garlic for 3–4 minutes until softened. Add the potato and mushrooms and fry for 5 minutes, stirring occasionally.

Pour in the stock, add the thyme, bay leaf and seasoning, and bring to the boil. Then reduce the heat and cook for 10–15 minutes until the veg are tender. Remove the bay leaf and thyme, transfer to a blender and blitz until smooth. Return to the pan, stir in the crème fraîche and gently reheat before serving.

Magic Weight-loss Soup

I can call this soup magic, and I will call it magic, because if I have a small bowl of it before every meal I can magically eat half as much as I would have done when I was a major binger!

76 Calories | 2.9g Fat | 0.4g Saturates | 3.8g Sugars | 1.2g Salt

SERVES 4

2 teaspoons olive oil

1 onion, finely chopped

1 garlic clove, finely chopped

$^1/_2$ head of celery, finely
   chopped

1 whole head of broccoli

1 vegetable stock cube in 650ml
   boiling water

Heat the oil in a saucepan over a medium heat. Add the onion and garlic and fry for 3–4 minutes until softened. Then stir in the celery.

Cut the broccoli into small florets and add to the pan. Pour in the vegetable stock, bring to the boil and simmer for 10 minutes. Transfer to a blender and blitz until smooth. Eat throughout the day whenever you are hungry.

Tip

Sip herbal and fruit teas between meals to stay hydrated and binge on body-cleansing foods, such as celery, grapefruit and rocket.

Parsnip + Apple Soup

Parsnips have such a unique, subtle flavour that it amazes me that I even considered adding curry powder to this recipe. Had I taken leave of my senses? But, guess what, the spices actually enhance rather than mask the flavour of the parsnips. Is there no end to my genius?!

246 Calories | 5.6g Fat | 0.8g Saturates | 18.5g Sugars | 1.7g Salt

SERVES 4

1 tablespoon olive oil

1 onion, chopped

2 teaspoons medium curry powder

6 large parsnips, peeled and roughly chopped

2 apples (Granny Smith if possible), peeled, cored and chopped

1¼ litres hot chicken or vegetable stock

sea salt and freshly ground black pepper

Heat the oil in a large saucepan or casserole over a gentle heat and fry the onion for 5 minutes. Stir in the curry powder and fry until the aroma is released. Then add the parsnips and place the lid on the pan. Sweat the vegetables over a low heat for a further 5 minutes. Add the apples and stock. Bring to the boil, then reduce the heat and simmer for 20 minutes until the vegetables are tender.

Remove the pan from the heat, pour the contents into a blender and whizz until smooth. Return the soup to the pan and gently reheat. Check the seasoning before serving.

Chicken Noodle Soup

This soup, made with a whole chicken and lots of veg to ensure maximum flavour, really does cure all ills. As my lovely dad always says, chicken soup soothes the soul as well as the stomach!

343 Calories | 11.9g Fat | 3.1g Saturates | 1.8g Sugars | 0.3g Salt

SERVES 8

FOR THE STOCK

2 onions, quartered

2 carrots, peeled and chopped

4 celery sticks, chopped

2 bay leaves

10 black peppercorns

1 bouquet garni

2 chicken stock cubes

1.2kg whole chicken

FOR THE SOUP

1/2 teaspoon olive oil

2 leeks, trimmed and sliced

200g mixed mushrooms, sliced

100g sweetcorn

100g vermicelli rice noodles

a handful of fresh flat-leaf
   parsley, chopped

Put all the stock ingredients, including the chicken, in a very large saucepan. Pour in as much cold water as needed to cover the ingredients, then bring to the boil. Reduce the heat to a simmer and cook for 1 1/2 hours. Every 20 minutes or so skim the froth off the top.

Remove the chicken and leave it to cool on a plate. Strain the stock through a sieve and set aside to cool. Let the fat rise to the top and, using a spoon, skim the fat off.

Now pour the oil into the same pan and fry the leeks, then the mushrooms for 3–5 minutes until softened. Then pour in the stock, bring it to the boil and add the sweetcorn. Reduce the heat and simmer for 8–10 minutes.

Take the chicken meat off the bone, discard the bones and skin, and add the chicken to the soup along with the rice noodles. Cook for 5–8 minutes until the noodles are cooked through. Stir in the parsley and serve.

Beautiful BLT

And now, folks, time for my all-time favourite sandwich, the great BLT, but without the guilt! When I think how I used to make these babies with spoonfuls of mayo, it makes me shudder. No wonder my little black dress felt sooooo little! Well, not anymore – chuck me an avocado!

306 Calories | 15.4g Fat | 4.8g Saturates | 2.6g Sugars | 3.1g Salt

SERVES 4

1 small avocado, peeled and
   stoned

7 slices of back bacon

2 tomatoes, chopped

8 slices of rye, wholemeal or
   granary bread, lightly toasted

8 romaine or iceberg lettuce
   leaves, shredded

sea salt and freshly ground
   black pepper

Mash the avocado in a bowl. Grill the bacon, then remove all the fat and, using scissors or a sharp knife, cut the bacon into thin strips. Add to the bowl with the mashed avocado. Stir in the chopped tomatoes. Season with a little salt and black pepper.

Divide between four slices of lightly toasted bread and top with the lettuce. Sandwich together with the other four slices of toasted bread.

Chicken + Avocado Wraps

What's to say? Avocado, chicken, mayo and tortillas… is that angels I can hear singing?

414 Calories | 16.4g Fat | 3.6g Saturates | 3.5g Sugars | 1.4g Salt

SERVES 4

4 tablespoons light mayonnaise

4 small wholemeal tortillas

1 red pepper, thinly sliced

350g skinless cooked chicken

1/2 iceberg lettuce, shredded

1 small avocado, peeled, stoned
  and sliced

12–16 fresh basil leaves

sea salt and freshly ground
  black pepper

Spread 1 tablespoon of mayonnaise on each tortilla, then divide the red pepper, chicken, lettuce and avocado between the tortillas. Season and add 3–4 basil leaves per wrap. Roll up and munch.

Tip

There's no denying that avocados are high in fat, but it's the good kind that helps lower cholesterol, and there's only a little used here!

Leabharlanna Poiblí Chathair Bhaile Átha Cliath
Dublin City Public Libraries

Celery, Carrot + Hummus Wraps

This is one of those wraps that leaves me feeling super-charged and ready for anything… well apart from housework. God I hate housework! You can of course double the hummus, ditch the bread and dip the veg if you want to be saintly.

332 Calories | 7.9g Fat | 1.1g Saturates | 6.5g Sugars | 0.6g Salt

SERVES 4

4 small wholemeal pitta breads

1 raw beetroot, grated

1 carrot, peeled and grated

4 celery sticks, cut into thin
   strips

a large handful of rocket
   or watercress

FOR THE HUMMUS

400g can chickpeas

$^{1}/_{2}$ red pepper, deseeded and
   chopped

juice of 1 lemon

1 garlic clove, crushed

2 tablespoons tahini

a good pinch of salt

To make the hummus, tip the chickpeas and their liquid into a pan and heat for 2 minutes. Then drain but reserve the liquid. Put the chickpeas, red pepper, lemon juice, garlic, tahini, salt and 2 tablespoons of the reserved cooking liquid (add a bit more if you like a thinner hummus) into a food processor and blitz until smooth.

Heat the pitta breads until soft, then split open and load in the hummus, beetroot, carrot, celery and rocket or watercress. And of course, an extra green salad on the side would be fabulous if you can be bothered!

Cheese +
Onion Sandwich

This tastes so naughty it shouldn't really be allowed… but we're allowed because I've swapped most of the high-fat cheese for low-fat cottage cheese but still left enough in so it tastes great too!

282 Calories | 9.6g Fat | 5.2g Saturates | 4.2g Sugars | 1.6g Salt

SERVES 1

3 tablespoons low-fat cottage
    cheese

1 tablespoon grated mature
    Cheddar

1 spring onion, finely chopped

1 celery stick, finely chopped

freshly ground black pepper

2 lettuce leaves

2 slices of granary or wholemeal
    bread

Put the cottage cheese, Cheddar, spring onion, celery and black pepper in a bowl and mix well. Lay the lettuce on one slice of bread, pile the cheese mixture on top and then lay the other slice of bread on top. Eat with a bowl of Magic Weight-loss Soup (page 56) if you've got some on the stove.

Tip

Water is a godsend for reducing toxins in your body. Make sure you drink at least 2 litres a day if you want to look luscious in your little black number.

Asian Lettuce Wraps

These are so lovely for a girls' night in, with maybe a cocktail too?

226 Calories | 10.9g Fat | 3.8g Saturates | 8.5g Sugars | 1.2g Salt

SERVES 4

$^{1}/_{2}$ tablespoon olive oil

300g extra-lean beef mince

1 onion, chopped

2 garlic cloves, chopped

2.5cm piece of fresh ginger, peeled and chopped

2 tablespoons hoisin sauce

1 tablespoon dark or light soy sauce

2 little gem lettuces, split into 10–20 leaves

2 carrots, peeled and grated

1 tablespoon roasted peanuts, chopped

1 spring onion, chopped

sea salt and freshly ground black pepper

Heat the oil in a heavy-based pan and fry the minced beef for 3–4 minutes over a medium heat until browned, breaking it up as you go. Season with a little salt and lots of black pepper, then remove from the heat and set it aside on a plate. Then in the same pan, fry the onion, garlic and ginger for about 2 minutes, then return the meat to the pan. Stir in the hoisin and soy sauces and cook for 2 more minutes, stirring all the time.

To serve, divide the lettuce leaves between four plates, spoon the chilli into each leaf and top with the carrots, peanuts and spring onion.

Nutty
Fish Salad

My husband always says he wants two salmon fillets
if we are having salmon for dinner (you know, the
whole omega-3 fat thing), but he doesn't actually
like salmon so it's always left over. Luckily I have
a plan…

401 Calories | 28.9g Fat | 4.5g Saturates | 1.4g Sugars | 1.5g Salt

SERVES 1

1 teaspoon olive oil

a squeeze of lemon juice

a large handful of mixed salad
   leaves

120g cooked salmon

10 raw whole pistachio nuts

sea salt and freshly ground black
   pepper

In a salad bowl, mix together the oil and lemon juice and
season well. Then add the salad leaves and toss well. Transfer
to a plate, lay the salmon on top and sprinkle over the
pistachio nuts to serve.

Tip

*Fill up on healthy proteins such as chicken, fish, eggs, nuts
and seeds, and lots of non-starchy veg – you'll be less likely
to accidentally consume that bar of chocolate screaming
your name…*

Five-star Turkey Club Sandwich

Make yourself one of these, go out in the garden and lie on the sun lounger (yes, even if it's raining), close your eyes and imagine you're in a top hotel – then devour the lot!

438 Calories | 5.5g Fat | 1.5g Saturates | 10.1g Sugars | 1g Salt

SERVES 1

6 slices of cucumber

$\frac{1}{2}$ apple, grated

1 spring onion, finely chopped

1 tablespoon fat-free Greek
   yogurt or light mayonnaise

6–8 fresh basil leaves

$\frac{1}{2}$ little gem or baby gem
   lettuce, shredded

2 slices of wholemeal or granary
   bread

a handful of rocket

1 ripe tomato, sliced

150g cooked roast turkey

sea salt and freshly ground
   black pepper

Put the cucumber, apple, spring onion, yogurt or mayonnaise, basil and lettuce in a bowl and mix well. Season with a little salt and black pepper.

Toast the bread, then spoon the yogurt mixture onto one slice. Layer on the rocket, tomato and turkey and sandwich together with the other slice.

Lemon Pepper Tuna Sandwich

Ha, ha, ha – I know what you're thinking – it can't be a proper sandwich if there's only one slice of bread, but remember that LBD picture and yourself in it, feeling just wonderful…

304 Calories | 6.7g Fat | 1.2g Saturates | 3.8g Sugars | 2g Salt

SERVES 1

100g canned tuna in spring
water, drained

1 tablespoon light mayonnaise

1 spring onion, finely chopped

$^{1}/_{2}$ green pepper, diced

zest of $^{1}/_{2}$ lemon, plus
1 tablespoon juice

a handful of rocket

1 small slice of wholemeal
bread

In a small bowl, mix the tuna with the other filling ingredients. Toast the bread and pile the ingredients on top. Serve with a bowl of Magic Weight-loss Soup (page 56).

Tip

Sit down when you eat – even if it's just a sandwich! You'd be amazed how many more calories you consume whilst standing and stuffing your face.

Courgetti Puttanesca

Who was the clever little so-and-so who invented the spiraliser? Come here and let me kiss you, whoever you are, because although I doubted I would, I do actually love courgetti spaghetti! Who'd have thunk it! No carbs and hardly any calories!

162 Calories | 6.7g Fat | 1.1g Saturates | 9.8g Sugars | 1.4g Salt

SERVES 4

1 tablespoon olive oil

2 garlic cloves, chopped

2 anchovy fillets

400g can peeled plum
   tomatoes

3 tablespoons chopped fresh
   flat-leaf parsley

1 tablespoon capers, drained

20 black pitted kalamata olives

1 teaspoon chopped red chilli
   (optional)

6–8 large courgettes, spiralised
   or cut into ribbons using
   a peeler

freshly ground black pepper

Heat a large, heavy-based frying pan over a medium heat and add the oil. Throw in the garlic and anchovies, and cook while stirring with a wooden spoon to break down the anchovies until they have practically dissolved in the oil.

Tip in the tomatoes and fry them while breaking them down with the spoon. Then stir in the parsley, capers, olives, a twist or two of black pepper and the chilli, if using. Simmer for 10–15 minutes until the liquid has evaporated. Stir in the courgetti spaghetti and cook for 1–2 minutes until softened.

Cauliflower Power Pizza

I howled with laughter when this was first suggested to me. I'm laughing on the other side of my face now as it satisfies without bloating and tastes delicious.

348 Calories | 23.8g Fat | 5.1g Saturates | 5.8g Sugars | 2.1g Salt

SERVES 4

FOR THE PIZZA

1 medium cauliflower

1 teaspoon dried herbs, such as
    oregano or thyme

1 egg

100g ground almonds

1 tablespoon grated Parmesan

olive oil spray

sea salt and freshly ground black
    pepper

FOR THE TOPPING

250g passata

any fresh or dried herbs

4 slices of lean ham, shredded

a matchbox-sized piece of
    half-fat Cheddar, grated

1 tablespoon grated Parmesan

Preheat the oven to 220°C/gas mark 7. Break the cauliflower into florets, cutting off most of the stalks, then blitz in a blender until it resembles fine breadcrumbs. (If you haven't got a blender or just like hard work, you can grate it.)

Either put the cauliflower in a covered bowl and microwave on high for 4 minutes, stirring halfway through, or steam it for 5–6 minutes until soft. Tip out onto a clean tea towel and leave until cool enough to handle. Now gather up the tea towel and keep squeezing it until all the water has drained out of the cauliflower – very important if you want a nice crispy pizza and not a soggy mess!

Mix the remaining pizza ingredients in a large bowl and add the cauliflower. Spray a baking tray with a little oil and press the pizza mixture out into a thin 23cm circle. Bake for about 20 minutes. Check to see that it's turned a lovely golden brown, then turn it over and cook for a further 10 minutes.

Remove from the oven and spoon the passata over the pizza crust, then load on the remaining toppings and bake for 8–10 minutes, or until hot and melty.

Salmon Penne Pasta Salad

Now don't freak out when you read 'wholewheat pasta'. It's never going to taste as great as the great white, but the usual white will not serve you well. It will raise your blood sugar and then make it crash back down, leaving you hungrier than ever.

437 Calories | 19.9g Fat | 3.1g Saturates | 2.8g Sugars | 1.6g Salt

SERVES 4

FOR THE PASTA

225g wholewheat penne pasta

400g can salmon

3 sun-dried tomatoes in oil,
   drained and chopped

a handful of fresh flat-leaf
   parsley, chopped

1/2 small red onion or 2 spring
   onions, finely chopped, to
   garnish (optional)

FOR THE DRESSING

2 tablespoons olive oil

2 tablespoons lemon juice

zest of 1/2 lemon

sea salt and freshly ground black
   pepper

Cook the penne according to the packet instructions. Drain the salmon and mix together with the remaining pasta ingredients. Whisk the dressing ingredients together in a small bowl. Stir the salmon into the pasta along with the dressing.

Tip

Have a laugh. Belly laughing strengthens abdominal muscles and also releases stress-burning, feel-good endorphins.

Greedy Girls Love Carbs Pasta Salad

If I could, I would put toasted pine nuts on absolutely everything; I once had a massive binge-out on them – I think I had about three bags all to myself! Sometimes a girl just wants carbs, but as there is little protein in this don't have it more than once a week.

387 Calories | 11.3g Fat | 1.3g Saturates | 8.6g Sugars | 1.2g Salt

SERVES 4

300g wholewheat penne pasta

2 tablespoons pine nuts

$\frac{1}{2}$ bunch of fresh mint leaves, chopped

16 pitted black olives

16 cherry tomatoes

4 teaspoons raisins

FOR THE DRESSING

1 tablespoon olive oil

1 tablespoon white balsamic vinegar, or any vinegar you like

sea salt and freshly ground black pepper

Cook the pasta according to the packet instructions, then drain and run under cold water.

Put the pasta in a bowl while you dry-fry the pine nuts in a non-stick pan. Now add them to the pasta along with the mint, olives, tomatoes and raisins.

In a small bowl, mix together the olive oil, vinegar, salt and black pepper, and pour over the pasta.

Baked Sea Bass with Tomato Pesto Salad

This is a lovely choice for lunch with friends in the garden – oh so posh!

206 Calories | 7.8g Fat | 0.9g Saturates | 1.8g Sugars | 0.3g Salt

SERVES 4

8 large vine tomatoes, thickly
   sliced

4 x 150g sea bass fillets

a squeeze of lemon juice

6–8 sprigs of fresh thyme

1 tablespoon green pesto

$\frac{1}{2}$ tablespoon olive oil

a large handful of fresh basil
   leaves

sea salt and freshly ground
   black pepper

Preheat the oven to 200°C/gas mark 6. Lay the tomato slices on a plate, sprinkle with a little salt and leave for the juices to come out of the tomatoes (I like to do this rather than use vinegar, which I think spoils the flavour).

Place the sea bass fillets on a baking tray lined with foil. Squeeze a little lemon juice on each one, sprinkle with black pepper and the sprigs of thyme. Cover tightly with foil and bake for 6–8 minutes.

Meanwhile, mix together the pesto and oil with $\frac{1}{2}$ tablespoon cold water. Drizzle this over the tomatoes, then scatter the basil leaves over the top. Serve with the fish and, of course (you know what I'm going to say), a green salad would go nicely with this too!

Grilled Mushroom Burgers

I am assured by every carnivore I've ever served this to that they've enjoyed it almost as much as a beef burger. Well, I'm not going to lie to you!

179 Calories | 12.2g Fat | 4g Saturates | 2.8g Sugars | 2.1g Salt

SERVES 4

2 tablespoons dark or light
  soy sauce

1 tablespoon olive oil

1 teaspoon freshly ground
  black pepper

$^1/_4$ teaspoon sea salt

4 large portobello mushrooms

100g reduced-fat cheese, grated

8 large lettuce leaves

4 slices of red onion

4 thick slices of tomato

1 avocado, stoned and thinly
  sliced

In a large bowl, whisk together the soy sauce, oil, black pepper and salt. Put the mushrooms in a baking dish and pour the sauce over the top. Leave to marinate for 30 minutes, turning now and again.

Once marinated, heat up the grill to nice and hot and grill the mushrooms for 3–4 minutes on each side until tender. Then top each mushroom with one-quarter of the cheese and allow it to melt.

Lay four lettuce leaves on a serving platter or board and pile a mushroom, one slice of onion, one slice of tomato and one-quarter of the avocado slices into each leaf. Top with another lettuce leaf and you are good to go.

Waldorf Salad Jackets

It's been years since I've had a Waldorf salad. They were all the rage in the eighties, so let's take a trip back to the eighties, girls! Shoulder pads anyone?

264 Calories | 11.6g Fat | 1.6g Saturates | 7.4g Sugars | 1.9g Salt

SERVES 4

4 baking potatoes or sweet
   potatoes no bigger than the
   palm of your hand

sea salt

FOR THE SALAD

4 tablespoons light mayonnaise

2 tablespoons natural yogurt

a squeeze of lemon juice

2 red apples, cored and diced
   (not peeled)

200g celery, chopped

2 tablespoons chopped walnuts

a large handful of chopped
   iceberg lettuce

Preheat the oven to 200°C/gas mark 6. Prick the potatoes with a fork, then wet them and sprinkle them with salt. Bake for 45 minutes–1 hour. Meanwhile, make the dressing by mixing the mayonnaise, yogurt and lemon juice together.

When the potatoes are ready, remove them from the oven. Put the apples, celery, walnuts and lettuce in a bowl. Pour the dressing on top and give the salad a good mix. Now split open the jacket potatoes and divide the salad equally between the potatoes and serve.

Shirley Valentine Salad

I never eat Greek salad without thinking of *Shirley Valentine*. For those of you who have never heard of *Shirley Valentine* and think I've taken leave of my senses, it's a movie about a woman who ran away from her boring life in Liverpool to find love… and feta cheese in Greece.

187 Calories | 10.5g Fat | 3g Saturates | 7.6g Sugars | 1g Salt

SERVES 4

FOR THE DRESSING

2 tablespoons olive oil

2 tablespoons red wine vinegar

zest of 1 lemon

sea salt and freshly ground
   black pepper

FOR THE SALAD

16 pitted black olives

4 large tomatoes, cut into
   eighths

1 onion, thinly sliced in circles

1 large romaine or cos lettuce

200g light feta cheese

1 cucumber, chopped into cubes

1 teaspoon dried oregano

1 teaspoon dried mint

In a small bowl, mix all the dressing ingredients together (super simple, huh?!). Put all the salad ingredients, except the oregano and mint, into a serving bowl. Pour over the dressing, sprinkle the herbs on top and toss well.

Tip

If you have a lapse, don't beat yourself up. Just refocus on your goal and get going again.

Chilli Beef

I make this when I have spare time on a Sunday and then divide it into six portions that I can freeze. Then, when I want to take a lunch to work, I can just pop it in the microwave. Ping! Angel wings!

313 Calories | 10g Fat | 3.5g Saturates | 7.1g Sugars | 0.4g Salt

SERVES 6

1 tablespoon vegetable oil

1 onion, chopped

2–4 garlic cloves, crushed

2 red chillies, finely chopped
(and deseeded if you don't
like it too spicy)

1 teaspoon ground cumin

2 tablespoons tomato purée

450g extra-lean beef mince

2 x 400g cans peeled plum
tomatoes

2 x 400g cans pinto beans,
drained

a handful of fresh coriander,
finely chopped

fat-free Greek yogurt, to serve

brown rice and salad, to serve
(optional)

Heat the oil in a large, heavy-based pan, then throw in the onion and garlic. Cook for 3–6 minutes until softened, stirring occasionally – you want the onion to be translucent, not coloured.

Next, stir in the chillies and cumin and cook for 1 minute, stirring constantly. Then add the tomato purée and cook for a further minute while stirring. Then add the beef mince, increase the heat a little and cook for about 5 minutes, breaking it up with the spoon as you go, then tip in the tomatoes with their juice. Bring to the boil over a high heat, reduce to a simmer and cook for about 30 minutes. Add the beans and cook for a further 10 minutes.

Serve in a bowl with 1 tablespoon of Greek yogurt. You could have a couple of tablespoons of brown rice or a salad alongside.

Veggie Coconut Soup

More often than not when I have a hangover I also have a bucket-load of guilt too. This Buddha-like dish helps ease it just a little.

197 Calories | 11g Fat | 6.7g Saturates | 11.7g Sugars | 0.8g Salt

SERVES 4

$^1/_2$ tablespoon coconut or
   vegetable oil

1 large onion, roughly chopped

2–4 teaspoons red curry paste

2 garlic cloves, chopped

2.5cm piece of fresh ginger,
   peeled and chopped

1 teaspoon ground turmeric

400ml can light coconut milk

1 vegetable stock cube dissolved
   in 100ml boiling water

1 tablespoon maple syrup
   (optional)

100–200g your favourite
   mushrooms, chopped

3 carrots, peeled and cut into
   thin strips

4 courgettes, spiralised into
   spaghetti (or cut into strips)

Heat the oil in a large saucepan or wok and fry the onion for 2–3 minutes until softened. Then add the curry paste, garlic, ginger and turmeric. Pour in the coconut milk and vegetable stock and give it a good stir. Bring to the boil, stir in the maple syrup (if using), then reduce the heat. Simmer over a very low heat for 10 minutes.

Drop in the mushrooms and carrots and cook for 3–5 minutes until softened. I put the courgettes in for the last couple of minutes, just to soften.

Courgette Fritters

This is great as a light lunch or as a side at dinnertime.

136 Calories | 8.7g Fat | 3.4g Saturates | 3.4g Sugars | 0.8g Salt

SERVES 4

1 egg

50g finely grated Parmesan

4 courgettes, grated

1 tablespoon olive oil

zest of 1 lemon, plus a small
    squeeze of juice

sea salt and freshly ground black
    pepper

Whisk the egg and Parmesan together in a large bowl. Mix in the courgettes, then shape into eight walnut-sized balls and flatten them out.

Heat a non-stick frying pan over a medium heat, add the oil and fry the fritters for 2 minutes on each side until golden brown. Serve with a salad and a bowl of soup, such as my Magic Weight-loss Soup (page 56).

Tip

Improve your posture! Standing tall with your shoulders back and bottom in will make you look more trim.

Egg Jumble

It never ceases to amaze me that this dish can fill up someone as greedy as me, but it does. It's my 'go-to' dish when I come in starving and want to eat in minutes.

243 Calories | 15.9g Fat | 4g Saturates | 1.6g Sugars | 1.3g Salt

SERVES 1

2 eggs

salt and freshly ground black

  pepper

1 teaspoon olive oil

6–8 your favourite mushrooms,

  sliced

1 slice of ham, chopped

1 tablespoon chopped fresh

  flat-leaf parsley

4–6 cherry tomatoes, chopped

Whisk the eggs and season, then set aside. Heat the oil in a frying pan and fry the mushrooms for 2 minutes, stirring constantly, then add the ham and fry for about 1 minute.

Now pour in the eggs and stir in the parsley and tomatoes and cook to your liking. Serve with a large green salad or your favourite vegetables alongside.

Dinner

Chicken Tickle Tikka

Tickle your taste buds with this guilt-free tikka. I've replaced the rice with my delicious Indian slaw – lots of lovely lean protein and three of your seven-a-day.

220 Calories | 6.8g Fat | 1.3g Saturates | 9.9g Sugars | 1g Salt

SERVES 4

FOR THE CHICKEN

150g low-fat plain yogurt

1 tablespoon madras curry paste

1/2 onion, grated

1 garlic clove, crushed

1 teaspoon curry powder

4 skinless chicken breasts, cut
into 4cm chunks

a large handful of fresh coriander

FOR THE INDIAN SLAW

1/2 small white cabbage, very
finely shredded

2 carrots, peeled and cut into
into thin strips

1/2 red onion, very thinly sliced

2 teaspoons cumin seeds, dry-fried

1 tablespoon lemon juice

1 tablespoon olive oil

sea salt

Soak eight wooden skewers in a bowl of water for 20 minutes to stop them burning when grilling.

To make the Indian slaw, put the vegetables and cumin seeds in a large bowl. Mix the lemon juice, oil and a pinch of salt together to make the dressing. Pour over the slaw vegetables and leave to marinate for 1 hour.

For the chicken, mix the yogurt, curry paste, onion, garlic and curry powder in a mixing bowl. Then add the chicken breasts and coriander and leave to marinate for at least 10 minutes and for up to two days in the fridge.

When you are ready to cook, heat the grill to medium, shake off any excess marinade, then thread equal portions of chicken onto the eight pre-soaked skewers. Cook under the grill for 10–15 minutes, turning now and again until cooked through.

Serve with the Indian slaw alongside.

Chicken
+ Noodles

Stop! Don't throw that leftover chicken out – make this lovely dish instead and, double bonus, even the kids will eat it.

531 Calories | 16.2g Fat | 3.2g Saturates | 6.1g Sugars | 2.2g Salt

SERVES 4

300g soba noodles

3 tablespoons reduced-fat
    peanut butter

3 tablespoons lime juice

2 teaspoons good-quality maple
    syrup

3 tablespoons dark or light
    soy sauce

1 tablespoon sesame oil

300g cooked chicken, shredded

1 small red pepper, thinly sliced

2 spring onions, shredded

2 tablespoons chopped fresh
    coriander

2 teaspoons toasted sesame
    seeds, to garnish

Cook the noodles according to the packet instructions, then drain and set aside to cool until lukewarm. In a food processor, blitz together the peanut butter, lime juice, maple syrup and 2 tablespoons of warm water until smooth to make the dressing.

Put the noodles and the remaining ingredients in a large bowl. Pour over the dressing. Toss well and finish with a flourish of sesame seeds. Serve with some steamed pak choi, broccoli or green beans, or all of them.

Roasted Garlic Chicken

Comfort food from the gods – garlicky roast chicken with a twist. Read on to see how I get the juiciest breast ever without lashings of fat. How to have a healthier roast? I always cook my chicken with the skin on but hurl it into the bin before I get the chance to scoff it! The skin is the devil's work!

299 Calories | 7.1g Fat | 1.7g Saturates | 3.3g Sugars | 1.2g Salt

SERVES 6

(OR 4 WITH LEFTOVERS FOR CHICKEN WRAPS)

1 tablespoon olive oil

1.6kg whole chicken

2 teaspoons dried mixed herbs

4 small onions, skins on, halved

2 carrots, peeled and chopped

2 celery sticks, cut into 4 pieces

6 garlic cloves, peeled

150ml hot chicken stock

sea salt and freshly ground black pepper

Preheat the oven to 240°C/gas mark 9. Drizzle the oil over the chicken, season well with salt and black pepper, and rub in and sprinkle the herbs over the top.

Put the bird breast-side down in a large roasting tray and scatter the onions, carrots, celery and garlic around the bird. Roast for 15 minutes.

Pour the stock on top of the vegetables (but not over the chicken) and reduce the heat to 200°C/gas mark 6. After 30 minutes, turn the chicken over to allow the breast to brown. Baste with the juices from the tin and cook for a further 30 minutes. Then pierce the chicken in the thigh with a skewer and if the juices run clear, take it out of the oven (if they don't, put it back in the oven for a further 10 minutes) and rest for 15 minutes.

Serve with your favourite steamed vegetables and a sweet jacket potato, Saintly Sage + Onion Balls (page 98) or Roast Jacket Potatoes (page 98).

Roast Jacket Potatoes

Yes, you read it right. Roast jacket potatoes – two great tastes in one fell swoop. Greedy girl heaven.

149 Calories | 1.8g Fat | 0.2g Saturates | 0.7g Sugars | 0.5g Salt

SERVES 4

4 medium potatoes

sea salt

Preheat the oven to 200°C/gas mark 6. Wash the potatoes and leave them wet, then sprinkle with sea salt (the water will help the salt to stick). Put them skin-side down straight onto the oven rack and bake for 45 minutes–1 hour.

Saintly Sage + Onion Balls

Saintly balls… just what you always wanted!

66 Calories | 3.6g Fat | 1.1g Saturates | 0.7g Sugars | 0.1g Salt

SERVES 4

4 tablespoons sage and onion
  stuffing

1 small onion, grated or
  very finely chopped

200g lean pork mince

a small handful of fresh parsley,
  finely chopped

zest of 1 small lemon

Preheat the oven to 200°C/gas mark 6. In a large bowl, mix together the sage and onion stuffing with 4–6 tablespoons of boiling water. Leave to cool and then add the remaining ingredients and mix well.

Form into eight balls, place on a baking tray and cook for 30–35 minutes, or until light golden in colour. Serve with the Roasted Garlic Chicken (page 97).

Chicken in Black Bean Sauce

If you ordered this from your local Chinese restaurant it would have double the oil and double the calories, so enjoy this healthy version. I usually alternate between pork and chicken with this recipe… such a rebel, me!

176 Calories | 4.6g Fat | 0.8g Saturates | 3g Sugars | 0.9g Salt

SERVES 4

200ml chicken stock

2 teaspoons cornflour

$1/2$ tablespoon groundnut or vegetable (not olive) oil

1.25cm piece of fresh ginger, peeled and grated

2 large garlic cloves, finely chopped

150g your favourite mushrooms, finely sliced

4 spring onions, cut into 2cm pieces

1 red or green pepper, finely sliced

400g boneless, skinless chicken breasts, cut into thin strips

3 tablespoons black bean sauce

Put the chicken stock in a saucepan and bring it to the boil. Mix the cornflour with 3 tablespoons of cold water, then add to the hot stock and stir until the sauce is smooth. Remove from the heat and set aside.

Heat a wok over a medium heat until nice and hot, then add the oil and heat for about 30 seconds. Add the ginger and garlic and fry, stirring constantly, for 2 minutes, then add the mushrooms and fry for another minute, stirring constantly. Finally, throw in the spring onions and red or green pepper and cook, stirring constantly, for a further minute.

Add the chicken and black bean sauce, and give it a stir. Add the hot, thickened stock, stir again and simmer for 4–5 minutes until the chicken is cooked through.

Serve with 3 tablespoons of cooked brown rice, and, if you want to go super-lean, some courgetti spaghetti or steamed veg – broccoli would be nice.

Chicken 'Bruschettas'

OK, ok, enough applause now. I know this idea is nothing short of genius! We all love bruschetta, but with this bruschetta I have kicked the carbs to the kerb and made it with fabulous low-fat, protein-rich chicken breasts.

172 Calories | 2.2g Fat | 0.5g Saturates | 0.8g Sugars | 0.7g Salt

SERVES 4

4 skinless, boneless chicken
   breasts

olive oil spray

$1/2$ garlic clove, crushed

$1/4$ small red onion, very finely
   chopped

a handful of chopped fresh basil

green salad, to serve

sea salt and freshly ground black
   pepper

Put the chicken breasts on a flat surface, cover them with baking paper and bash with a rolling pin until they're all the same thickness.

Heat a non-stick frying pan (with a lid) over a medium heat. Spray the breasts on one side with oil and season well on both sides. Then put the chicken into the hot pan, oiled-side down, to sear until it turns white, then turn it over. Put a tight-fitting lid on the pan, reduce the heat and cook for 10 minutes over a very low heat – do not lift the lid. Remove from the heat, and still without lifting the lid, leave to rest for 10 minutes. This will give you perfectly cooked, moist chicken – if you follow the instructions exactly.

Meanwhile, mix together all the remaining ingredients and season with salt and black pepper. Pile the mixture onto the chicken breasts and serve with a large green salad.

Pork Souvlaki with Nutty Rice + Winter Slaw

If only I could take my own advice and remember to marinate this overnight. It still tastes delicious if I don't, but not quite as good.

428 Calories | 12.6g Fat | 2.4g Saturates | 6.8g Sugars | 1.4g Salt

SERVES 4

FOR THE PORK SOUVLAKI

juice of 1 lemon

1 garlic clove, crushed

2 teaspoons dried oregano

1 teaspoon dried mint (optional)

1 tablespoon olive oil

400g leg of pork, all fat removed
   and cut into 2cm squares

salt and freshly ground black
   pepper

Nutty Rice (page 104) and/or
   Winter Slaw (page 104),
   to serve

To make the pork souvlaki, mix together all the ingredients, except the pork, in a non-metallic bowl. Stir in the pork pieces. Leave to marinate in the fridge for at least 6 hours or overnight if possible.

To make the nutty rice and winter slaw, see page 104.

When you are ready to cook the pork, soak eight bamboo skewers for at least 20 minutes and thread the pork pieces onto them. Preheat the grill to medium or, better still, heat a barbecue and cook for 4–8 minutes, turning halfway.

Serve with the nutty rice and winter slaw or, if you want to lose weight faster, just the slaw!

Nutty Rice + Winter Slaw

SERVES 4

FOR THE NUTTY RICE

200g brown basmati rice

500ml hot chicken stock

a handful of toasted cashews,
   almonds or pine nuts

FOR THE WINTER SLAW

$1/2$ red cabbage, finely sliced

$1/2$ white cabbage, finely sliced

1 red pepper, thinly sliced

$1/2$ red onion, thinly sliced

a large handful of fresh flat-leaf
   parsley, chopped

1 tablespoon white wine vinegar

1 tablespoon olive oil

1 tablespoon Greek yogurt

1 teaspoon Dijon mustard

To make the nutty rice, heat a saucepan (one that has a tight-fitting lid) over a medium heat, add the rice and pour over the stock. Bring to the boil, stir once, then reduce the heat to a low simmer and cover with the lid. Cook for 20 minutes without lifting the lid. Remove from the heat and leave the rice to sit for 10 minutes with the lid on. Stir in the nuts.

To make the slaw, put the red cabbage, white cabbage, red pepper, onion and parsley in a large bowl and mix. Then, in a separate jug, combine the vinegar, oil, yogurt and mustard. Pour over the slaw.

Tip

Stop for a minute before you eat something you shouldn't, and ask yourself what it is you really want – maybe it's emotional hunger and all you need is a hug!

Lean Lasagne

I'm your best friend ever as I have removed approximately 10 million calories from this lasagne by swapping fatty beef for lean minced pork and substituting a heavy, calorie-laden béchamel sauce for a lovely, light ricotta and Parmesan one. This is also a great meal for all the family.

551 Calories | 28.4g Fat | 14.8g Saturates | 11.8g Sugars | 1.5g Salt

SERVES 4

FOR THE RAGU

400g lean pork mince

1 tablespoon olive oil

1 medium onion, finely chopped

2 garlic cloves, finely chopped

2 carrots, peeled and finely
   chopped

2 tablespoons tomato purée

100ml red wine (optional)

400g can chopped tomatoes

1 bay leaf

sea salt and freshly ground
   black pepper

Heat a heavy-based frying pan over a medium heat and dry-fry the pork for 2 minutes until browned, stirring constantly. Remove from the heat and set aside. You will have to do this in batches if you don't have a very large pan, as the meat will steam rather than brown if overcrowded.

Heat the oil in the same pan and fry the onion and garlic for 3–5 minutes until softened. Then add the carrots and fry for about 1 minute. Then add the tomato purée and fry for 1 minute, stirring constantly. Now add the pork and pour in the wine, if using. Simmer for 2 minutes until the wine is reduced. Pour in the tomatoes and half-fill the empty can with cold water and add it to the pan. Increase the heat to a bubble, breaking up the tomatoes as you stir. Season well and add the bay leaf. Reduce the heat and simmer for about 30 minutes. (You can make this a couple of days in advance and keep in the fridge. You can also freeze it at this stage and keep for three weeks.)

FOR THE CHEESE SAUCE

AND LAYERS

1 egg

250g ricotta cheese

a large handful of fresh flat-leaf
    parsley, finely chopped

9 sheets of no pre-cook lasagne

150g ball mozzarella cheese
    (light if you can get it),
    roughly grated

50g Parmesan or Pecorino,
    grated

4 large tomatoes, sliced

To make the cheese sauce, break the egg into a bowl and mix together with the ricotta, parsley and a little salt and black pepper. Preheat the oven to 180°C/gas mark 4.

Now it's time to assemble your lasagne. Put one third of the meat sauce over the bottom of an ovenproof dish (roughly 25cm x 30cm x 6cm-deep) and then lay three lasagne sheets on top. Then spoon over half of the remaining meat sauce. Now lay three more lasagne sheets over the top of that, and spread with the remaining meat mixture. Lay the last three lasagne sheets on top and spoon the ricotta sauce over the top. Sprinkle with the grated mozzarella and Parmesan or Pecorino. Top with the sliced tomatoes. Cover with foil and bake for 40 minutes, removing the foil for the last 10 minutes of the cooking time.

Serve with a large green salad and a cheeky glass of red wine.

Burgers +
Sweet Potato Fries

Look, we know we all want to get into our little black dress but we don't want to go without our burgers do we? No, we most certainly DO NOT!

599 Calories | 21.6g Fat | 8.8g Saturates | 7.1g Sugars | 1.9g Salt

SERVES 4

FOR THE SWEET POTATO FRIES

3 sweet potatoes, cut into

   1cm thick chips

1 teaspoon cornflour

sea salt and freshly ground

   black pepper

FOR THE BURGERS

780g lean beef mince

1 onion, finely grated

a small bunch of fresh flat-leaf

   parsley finely chopped

1 tablespoon tomato purée

1 small slice of wholemeal

   bread, made into breadcrumbs

low-calorie oil spray

4 x 60g wholemeal rolls

Preheat the oven to 240°C/gas mark 9. Put the sweet potato fries onto a baking tray, spray with a little oil and sprinkle with the cornflour, salt and black pepper. Toss well. Bake for about 25 minutes, or until they are golden, turning halfway through.

Time to make the burgers! Preheat the grill to medium. Simply put all the burger ingredients in a bowl, then wet your hands (this will stop the meat sticking to them) and lightly combine the ingredients – don't overdo this as it will result in tough burgers. Gently shape into four patties and spray with a little oil, pop under the grill for 5–8 minutes until cooked just the way you like them, turning halfway through.

Serve in the wholemeal rolls with the sweet potato fries on the side and a large salad.

Cabbage Rolls with Pork + Rice

Sweet, tender cabbage, gorgeous garlic-infused rice, tender, juicy pork – this dish never fails to comfort me.

420 Calories | 17.6g Fat | 9g Saturates | 4.9g Sugars | 0.8g Salt

SERVES 4

185g pudding rice (white short-grain rice), washed and drained

250g pork mince

$1/2$ medium onion, finely chopped

2 large garlic cloves, finely sliced

1 medium tomato, grated

2 large pinches of dried sage

1 large Savoy cabbage (or better still, try to get one of those really large white cabbages from a Turkish shop, as they are not only very sweet-tasting, but much easier to separate)

50g butter, plus extra for greasing

sea salt and freshly ground black pepper

In a large bowl, mix the pudding rice with the pork, onion, garlic, tomato, sage and seasoning.

One by one, make a cut at the base of each cabbage leaf and pull the leaves gently off the cabbage, being careful not to split the leaf. Cut the bottom, very hard piece of stalk out, keeping the leaves intact.

Bring a large saucepan of water to the boil, and blanch the cabbage leaves a few at a time for about 1 minute until they begin to soften – don't overcook them. Remove from the heat and set aside.

When the leaves have cooled down a little, take each leaf and place about 1 tablespoon of the rice mix, squeezing the mix slightly in your hand, in a line on the side of the leaf closest to you, about 1cm from the edge. From the edge closest to you, now roll up the leaf tightly to form a cigar shape. You don't need to fold them in at the ends – the ends will naturally stick together when cooking.

Butter a deep, heavy-based saucepan (about. 25cm – Le Creuset type is ideal). Pack the cabbage rolls into the saucepan

Concentrate on your food. Eating while watching TV increases your chances of overindulging.

TO SERVE

1 large garlic clove, very
   finely chopped

2–3 tablespoons lemon juice

in layers. They shouldn't reach the top of the pan, as the rice will expand as they cook. Put a few dots of butter over the top of the leaves, cover with a piece of baking paper and top this with an upside-down heatproof plate small enough to fit inside the pan. If you have room in the saucepan to place a weight on top, so much the better.

Pour 1 cup of boiling salted water over the cabbage leaves. Put the saucepan over a high heat and, just as the water comes back up to the boil, reduce the heat to low. Cover with a lid and cook for 40–45 minutes, checking from time to time that the water hasn't evaporated. Add a little more if necessary. Remove the plate, weight and baking paper for the last 10 minutes of cooking time.

Meanwhile, put the garlic, lemon juice and 2–3 tablespoons of boiling water in a small jug and mix together.

Test a roll to make sure the rice is cooked, then place two pieces of kitchen paper on top of the leaves and put the lid back on. Leave for 15–20 minutes before removing the kitchen paper and carefully tipping the saucepan upside down onto a serving plate. (Don't worry if there's a little water remaining in the pan.) Put the lemon juice mixture on the table for people to help themselves.

Sesame Beef + Cucumber Noodles

I know what you're thinking, *cucumber* noodles? Has the woman gone mad? But, honestly, this is so delicious and we want/need/and would kill to get that dress zip to do up all the way to the top!

191 Calories | 11.8g Fat | 3g Saturates | 4.5g Sugars | 0.8g Salt

SERVES 4

250g feather steak

2 cucumbers

1 romaine lettuce, shredded

150g white cabbage, very finely shredded

2 spring onions, finely sliced

a handful of fresh coriander, roughly chopped

1 tablespoon olive oil

1 tablespoon toasted sesame oil

juice of 1 lime

1 teaspoon clear honey

1 teaspoon dark or light soy sauce

1 red chilli, finely chopped

1/2 tablespoon each of black and white sesame seeds

sea salt and freshly ground black pepper

Heat a heavy-based frying pan over a medium heat. Season the steak and fry for 2 minutes on each side for medium-rare. Remove from the pan and set aside to rest for at least 3–4 minutes.

Using a spiraliser or a julienne peeler, make the cucumbers into noodles. Cut the steak into thin strips and put in a large bowl together with the lettuce, cabbage, spring onions and coriander.

Put the oils, lime juice, honey, soy sauce and chilli in a bowl, whisk with a fork and pour onto the salad. Sprinkle the sesame seeds over the top.

Fish + Chips

You know, it's not the end of the world if we sometimes eat something that's been fried… there I've said it! Now this should be a real treat, not an everyday meal!

589 Calories | 20.4g Fat | 2.8g Saturates | 11.1g Sugars | 1.1g Salt

SERVES 4

FOR THE CHIPS

700g sweet potatoes (try to use
    all the same size)

2 tablespoons olive or coconut
    oil

sea salt

FOR THE FISH

500ml sunflower oil, for frying

1 egg white

50g self-raising flour, plus a little
    extra to coat the fish

50g cornflour

125ml ice-cold sparkling water

about. 700g white fish, cut into
    4 equal pieces

200g cooked petits pois, to serve

Preheat the oven to 200°C/gas mark 6. Wash the potatoes and cut into chips, then put them onto a large, shallow baking tray. Drizzle with the olive or coconut oil, sprinkle with salt and toss until evenly covered. Bake for 30 minutes, turning them over a couple of times during cooking.

Meanwhile, put the sunflower oil into a large, heavy-based, non-stick frying pan. Heat very slowly until hot. It's ready when a small cube of bread sizzles and turns golden. Do not put the fish into the oil until it's properly heated.

While the oil is heating, whisk the egg white until bubbly. Put the flour and cornflour in a bowl and pour in the sparkling water, whisking as you go. Then carefully mix in the egg white to make a smooth batter. Don't bash those bubbles out.

Dry the fish pieces on kitchen paper, sprinkle with a little flour, then dip them in the batter. Now gently lower them into the hot oil. Fry for 3 minutes on each side, or until golden brown. Remove them from the frying pan using a slotted spoon and drain on kitchen paper. Serve with the sweet potato chips and petits pois.

Bistro-style Mussels

I'm going to be kind to us girls – I reckon we need chips with this dish! I mean, really, mussels without chips?! Go to page 114 for my guilt-free chip recipe and make us all some!

438 Calories | 9.8g Fat | 2g Saturates | 7.9g Sugars | 4.3g Salt

SERVES 4

1/2 tablespoon olive oil

1 medium onion, finely chopped

6 garlic cloves, crushed

125ml white wine

1 tablespoon very finely
   chopped fresh coriander

750g passata

3–4 sprigs fresh thyme

1.75kg fresh mussels, scrubbed
   and debearded

410g can green lentils, rinsed
   and drained

a pinch of freshly ground black
   pepper

sea salt, if needed

In a large pot, heat the oil slowly until hot. Add the onion and garlic and cook, stirring occasionally, for about 5 minutes until the onion is translucent. Stir in the wine and simmer for 2–3 minutes. Add the coriander, passata and thyme. Reduce the heat and simmer, partially covered, for 25 minutes, stirring occasionally.

Discard any mussels that have broken shells or that don't clamp shut when tapped. Add the mussels to the pot. Cover with a lid and bring to the boil. Cook, shaking the pot occasionally, for about 3 minutes – just until the mussels open, . Remove the open mussels. If there are any mussels still closed, continue to boil, uncovering the pot as necessary to remove the mussels as soon as their shells open. Discard any that do not open. Stir in the lentils and allow them to heat through for 1–2 minutes.

Stir the black pepper into the broth. Taste the broth and, if needed, add salt. Ladle the broth over the mussels and serve.

Baked Mackerel, Fennel + Tomatoes

OK, it's oily fish time. I simply can't not include it in a book promoting healthy eating… Ha ha ha but how I wish I could!

366 Calories | 25g Fat | 5g Saturates | 3.7g Sugars | 1.3g Salt

SERVES 4

olive oil spray

1 large fennel bulb, top and
   bottom trimmed and bulb
   cut into eighths

2 teaspoons fennel seeds

1 garlic clove, finely chopped

400g passata

zest of 1 organic lemon (or at
   the very least, unwaxed)

4 x 150g small mackerel fillets

fresh basil or flat-leaf parsley,
   to garnish

sea salt and freshly ground
   black pepper

Preheat the oven to 200°C/gas mark 6. Spray a baking tray with oil, then scatter the fennel slices on top and spray them. Bake for 20–30 minutes until the fennel has softened.

While the fennel is baking, spray a medium frying pan with the oil, fry the fennel seeds for a few seconds, remove from the pan and in the same pan lightly fry the garlic for 2 minutes. Add the passata to the garlic and season well. Stir in the lemon zest and the reserved fennel seeds.

Once the fennel has softened, stir it into the passata mixture. Bring to a simmer and cook gently for 20 minutes.

While the passata is simmering, heat a griddle pan, season the mackerel fillets, spray them with oil and very gently griddle them skin-side down for 2–3 minutes until crisped up and cooked through.

Pour the passata mixture into a serving dish, lay the fillets on top and sprinkle with freshly torn basil or chopped parsley.

Veggie Curry in a Hurry

Oh boy, this is good, and on the table in under half an hour. Using lots of onion, garlic, curry paste and coconut milk really takes the rather bland chickpea to a whole new level, so it actually tastes delicious as well as being good for you.

285 Calories | 12g Fat | 6.7g Saturates | 4.4g Sugars | 1.8g Salt

SERVES 4

½ tablespoon olive oil

2 onions, sliced

4 garlic cloves, sliced

1 teaspoon ground cumin

1 teaspoon curry powder

2 tablespoons madras curry paste

3 potatoes, peeled and roughly chopped

400g can chickpeas, rinsed and drained

200ml hot vegetable or chicken stock

400ml can light coconut milk

300g fresh spinach

sea salt and freshly ground black pepper

Heat the oil in a large frying pan or wok (with a lid) and fry the onions and garlic until softened. Then add the cumin and curry powder and stir for 30 seconds. Add the curry paste and fry for 1 minute, then the potatoes, cooking for a further minute or so. Add the chickpeas, stock and some seasoning. Bring to the boil, then reduce the heat to a simmer, cover with a lid and leave to gently pop and bubble for 10 minutes. Remove the lid and cook for a further 20 minutes, or until the potatoes are cooked through.

Pour in the coconut milk and let it bubble for 1 minute. Then stir in the spinach. Serve with your favourite steamed green vegetables.

Tomato + Avocado Courgetti

I was one of the last people to be convinced about courgette spaghetti. I just refused to even try it, but now I hardly go a couple of days without eating it. It's no-carb, it's a green veg, it's filling but light at the same time – crikey, I think I'm in love!

230 Calories | 19.3g Fat | 4.4g Saturates | 3.5g Sugars | 0.8g Salt

SERVES 4

4 teaspoons olive oil

2 handfuls of your favourite
   cherry tomatoes

6 courgettes, spiralised

2 tablespoons grated Parmesan

FOR THE AVOCADO SAUCE

1 large ripe avocado, peeled and
   stoned

1 tablespoon olive oil

1 tablespoon white balsamic
   vinegar

$1/2$ teaspoon sea salt

1 garlic clove, crushed

juice of 1 lemon

2 teaspoons green pesto

Put all the avocado sauce ingredients in a blender and blend until smooth.

Heat a large, non-stick frying pan over a medium heat, add the oil and then the tomatoes. Cover with a lid, give the pan a good shake and cook for about 5 minutes. Remove the lid and add the courgettes, and stir for a few seconds until the courgette wilts.

Empty the pan into a large bowl, stir in the avocado sauce and Parmesan, and serve alongside a grilled chicken breast or a steamed white fish fillet. Or enjoy on its own for a lighter meal or lunch.

Teriyaki Chicken

Sticky, sweet and garlicky? Diet? What diet?

244 Calories | 7g Fat | 1.3g Saturates | 4.2g Sugars | 1.4g Salt

SERVES 1

4 small skinless and boneless
   chicken breasts, cut into cubes

3 tablespoons teriyaki sauce

1 tablespoon vegetable or
   coconut oil

2 garlic cloves, finely chopped

2 courgettes, cut into thin strips

2 carrots, cut into thin strips

4 spring onions, cut into thin
   strips

1 tablespoon sesame seeds,
   toasted

brown rice and steamed
   broccoli, to serve

Put the chicken into a bowl with the teriyaki sauce and leave to marinate in the fridge for at least 10 minutes or overnight if possible.

Then thread the chicken onto eight wooden skewers soaked for at least 30 minutes in warm water, or use metal ones. Preheat the grill to hot and cook the chicken for 4–8 minutes, turning occasionally.

Heat the oil in a wok or large frying pan and stir-fry the garlic for a couple of seconds before adding the courgettes, carrots and spring onions.

Scatter the sesame seeds over the grilled chicken and serve with the vegetables and 2 tablespoons brown rice per person with some steamed broccoli.

 Tip

Ditch the sit-ups. Crunches won't burn belly fat. Try some supercharged moves like squats and star jumps instead as they ramp up your metabolism and turn on fat-burning hormones! Try three sets of 10 once a day.

Cumin + Coriander Lamb

Fancy a trip to Morocco? Then serve this spiced lamb with my Exotic Carrot Salad (page 135).

306 Calories | 20.8g Fat | 8.3g Saturates | Trace Sugars | 0.9g Salt

SERVES 4

2 tablespoons ground cumin

2 tablespoons ground coriander

1 tablespoon paprika

1 tablespoon ground ginger

1 tablespoon finely ground black
   pepper

$^1/_4$ teaspoon sea salt

$^1/_2$ tablespoon olive oil

4 medium leg of lamb steaks,
   fat removed

roasted tomatoes and green
   beans, to serve

Mix together the cumin, coriander, paprika, ginger, black pepper, salt and oil and rub the mixture all over the lamb. Leave to marinate in the fridge for at least 10 minutes or overnight if possible.

When you're ready to eat, heat the grill until hot and grill the lamb for 5–10 minutes, turning halfway through, depending on the thickness of the lamb and how you like it cooked. Serve with roasted tomatoes and green beans.

Tip

If you feel hungry between meals eat almonds. Their fibre content means you're actually burning calories whilst eating them!

Bream
in a Parcel

My kids call this dish 'broom in a parcel', which
always makes me giggle! Gorgeous soft white fish
cooked in a parcel with fragrant herbs and a splash
of vino – yum!

267 Calories | 9.5g Fat | 0.4g Saturates | 3.7g Sugars | 1.1g Salt

SERVES 4

fennel or dill fronds, or a few
   fennel seeds (optional)
4 x 225g sea bream or sea bass
   fillets, skin on
1 red pepper, cut into thin strips
1 yellow pepper, cut into thin
   strips
2 small onions, very finely sliced
salt and freshly ground black
   pepper or, better still,
   mixed peppercorns
1 tablespoon olive oil
4 tablespoons white wine
   (optional)

Preheat the oven to 220°C/gas mark 7. Take a piece of
baking paper and a piece of foil slightly bigger – big enough
to fold over a fish fillet. You are going to lay the fillet in the
middle, so needs the paper to be big enough to fold over the
fillet comfortably with enough to scrunch up on all four sides.

Place the foil on the table with the baking paper and flick
some water over it. If you are using the fennel or dill, sprinkle
it on the paper first, then lay the fish on top. Scatter over the
red and yellow peppers and onions, fennel seeds, if using, and
a little salt and black pepper.

Drizzle over the oil and the wine too, if using. Carefully fold
the paper over the fish and fold and scrunch the edges of the
foil together so that the parcel is tightly sealed – you don't
want any steam to escape. Repeat for all four fillets.

Put the fish parcels in the oven and cook for 8–10 minutes.
Remove from the oven, place on a plate and carefully open
the parcel – the steam can be vicious!

Turkey Meatloaf

I know it's not a meatloaf but I don't care, I'm calling it one anyway!

254 Calories | 6.8g Fat | 3.1g Saturates | 2.8g Sugars | 0.8g Salt

SERVES 4–6

butter, for greasing

750g turkey mince

200g cooked brown rice

1 large carrot, peeled and grated

1 large courgette, grated

1 tomato, finely chopped

a small bunch of fresh flat-leaf
    parsley, finely chopped

1 onion, finely chopped

50g grated Parmesan

1 tablespoon tomato purée

1 egg, beaten

sea salt and freshly ground
    black pepper

Preheat the oven to 180°C/gas mark 4.

Grease a 1kg loaf tin with butter. Then simply mix all the other ingredients together and spoon into the loaf tin. Bake for 30–35 minutes. Serve with lots of steamed vegetables, such as cabbage.

Tip

Avoid rewarding yourself with food. It'll only end up feeling like a punishment when you can't get into your favourite dress!

Celeriac Cottage Pie

Poor old celeriac really does have a face only a mother could love. BUT it makes up for that because it can be used in any dish you would put potato in but only has 25 per cent of the calories of the naughty spud!

403 Calories | 21.2g Fat | 9.2g Saturates | 7.4g Sugars | 2.7g Salt

SERVES 4

600g lean steak mince

2 teaspoons olive oil

1 onion, finely chopped

4 celery sticks

2 carrots, peeled and chopped

1 bay leaf

salt and freshly ground black
   pepper

1 teaspoon tomato purée

2 beef stock cubes

300ml boiling water

FOR THE MASH

1 leek, trimmed and sliced

800g celeriac, peeled and cubed

100g half-fat crème fraîche

Heat a large frying pan over a medium heat and dry-fry the mince for 3–4 minutes, stirring constantly, then set aside.

Add the oil to the same pan over a low heat and cook the onion, celery and carrots for 4–6 minutes until soft. Return the mince to the pan and add the bay leaf, salt and black pepper, tomato purée, stock cubes and water. Bring to the boil, then reduce the heat, cover with a lid and simmer for 20–30 minutes, removing the lid for the last 10 minutes of cooking time.

To make the mash, boil the leeks and celeriac in salted water for 8–10 minutes until tender, then drain thoroughly, season to taste and mash with the crème fraîche.

Transfer the beef mixture to an ovenproof dish, top with the celeriac mash and pop under a medium grill for 5–8 minutes until golden.

Salmon + Asparagus en Papillote

Basically this is posh fish in a packet... ok, let's go back to salmon en papillote – it sounds so much more delicious.

324 Calories | 20.9g Fat | 5.5g Saturates | 0.8g Sugars | 0.8g Salt

SERVES 4

16 fine asparagus spears

4 x 150g thick salmon fillets

20g butter, melted

2 tablespoons Pernod, vermouth

  or dry white wine

1 lemon, quartered, to serve

sea salt and freshly ground

  black pepper

Preheat the oven to 200°C/gas mark 6. Take a piece of baking foil large enough to wrap all four salmon fillets in a loose parcel. Lay the asparagus spears in the middle of the foil and put the salmon on top, skin-side down. Brush with the melted butter. Pour over the Pernod, vermouth or wine, then season with salt and a very little black pepper.

Close the parcel, scrunching up the edges of the foil tightly, and place on the oven rack. Cook for about 15 minutes – leave to cool for about 1 minute before opening to check if the fillets are done.

Serve with a wedge of lemon on the side.

Mexican Rice

Sometimes only a steaming bowl of comforting spiced rice will do.

265 Calories | 5g Fat | 0.8g Saturates | 3.7g Sugars | 0.8g Salt

SERVES 4

1 tablespoon olive oil

1 onion, diced

1 garlic clove, chopped

1 red chilli, finely chopped

1 teaspoon ground cumin

1 green pepper, diced

1 tomato, deseeded and roughly
  chopped

70g frozen sweetcorn

4 tablespoons of tinned red
  kidney beans

200g brown basmati rice

240ml hot chicken stock
  (made with a stock cube)

a handful of fresh coriander,
  chopped

Heat the oil in a heavy-based, lidded saucepan and fry the onion for 4–6 minutes until softened. Then add the garlic, chilli, cumin and green pepper and cook for 2 minutes, stirring constantly.

Stir in the tomato, sweetcorn and kidney beans, then add the rice and give it all a stir. Pour in the stock, bring it to a bubble, then reduce the heat, cover with a lid and simmer for 30 minutes until the rice is tender. Top with the coriander.

Tip

Use small plates or bowls – it's an easy way to control portion size!

Lamb's Liver Arabic-style

This recipe is unashamedly stolen from my mum.
Liver is a great source of lean protein and let's face
it, there's only so much chicken any of us can eat!

255 Calories | 10.8g Fat | 2.3g Saturates | 4g Sugars | 1.3g Salt

SERVES 4–6

450g lamb's liver

1 tablespoon olive oil

1 medium onion, finely chopped

1 tablespoon plain flour mixed
   with salt, black pepper and
   1 teaspoon ground cumin

2 large garlic cloves,
   very finely chopped

2 teaspoons cumin seeds

150–200ml hot chicken
   or vegetable stock

1 tablespoon pomegranate
   molasses

2 tablespoons finely chopped
   fresh coriander

Rinse the liver and remove any gristly bits. Hopefully your
slices of liver are 1cm or more thick, so that you can cut them
into cubes, otherwise leave the liver in slices.

Heat the oil in a large heavy-based pan and gently fry the
onion for 3–5 minutes until soft.

While the onion is cooking, toss the liver in the flour mixture
– if your liver is cubed, the easiest way to do this is to put
everything in a plastic food bag and give it a good shake.
Once the onion has softened, add the garlic and cumin
seeds and cook for 1–2 minutes until the seeds start popping.
Transfer the contents of the pan to the bowl. You might need
to add a little oil to the pan if the pan is very dry, then add the
liver and fry until just browned – do not overcook it.

Mix the pomegranate molasses into the stock and add to the
pan together with the cooked onion, garlic and cumin seeds.
Give it a good stir and simmer for a further 3–5 minutes, but
don't let the liver become tough and overcooked. Stir in the
coriander and serve with the Exotic Carrot Salad (opposite) or
a green salad.

Exotic Carrot Salad

This is a gorgeous salad inspired by many visits to Marrakech and it works alongside just about anything, but goes particularly well with grilled fish, meat or chicken.

38 Calories | 1.9g Fat | 0.3g Saturates | 3.4g Sugars | 0.6g Salt

SERVES 4

4 carrots, peeled and very

thinly sliced (I use a mandolin)

$1/4$ teaspoon ground cumin

2 teaspoons olive oil

2 teaspoons vinegar

(I use sweet white balsamic)

2 teaspoons orange flower water

1 tablespoon chopped fresh

coriander or flat-leaf parsley

salt

Plunge the carrots into a saucepan of salted, boiling water and cook for 1 minute (you want them just softened, not cooked). Drain thoroughly and put into a salad bowl. Whisk the remaining ingredients in a small bowl and pour over the carrots.

Tip

It's best to leave yourself a good few hours between your last meal of the day and bedtime in order to give your body time to burn it off.

Desserts

Satsumas Dipped in Dark Chocolate

Emergency! Emergency! I neeeeeeeed chocolate
and I need it now! Voilà!

89 Calories | 4.4g Fat | 3.5g Saturates | 10.7g Sugars | Trace Salt

SERVES 4

4 satsumas

50g dark chocolate (about
   70 per cent cocoa solids)

desiccated coconut or sea salt
   (optional)

Lay a piece of baking paper on a baking tray. Peel and
separate the satsumas into segments.

Melt the chocolate in a bowl in the microwave or in a
heatproof bowl over a saucepan of barely simmering water.
Dip half of each satsuma segment into the chocolate and lay
on the baking paper.

If you are using the coconut or sea salt, sprinkle it over the
chocolate part of the satsumas and immediately place the tray
in the fridge for 10 minutes to harden the chocolate.

Vanilla + Pear Custard Tarts

Can somebody please make sure that whichever man, woman or child it was who invented light puff pastry gets knighted! Lower in calories with up to 30 per cent less fat than standard pastry, this lets you enjoy pudding without piling on the pounds.

117 Calories | 4.5g Fat | 2.2g Saturates | 6.4g Sugars | Trace Salt

MAKES 4 TARTS/

SERVES 4

1 large ripe pear

100g ready-rolled light puff
   pastry

4 tablespoons low-fat custard
   mixed with ½ teaspoon
   vanilla extract

milk, for brushing

½ teaspoon ground ginger
   mixed with 1 teaspoon icing
   sugar

Preheat the oven to 220°C/gas mark 7. Line a baking tray with baking paper. Cut the pastry into four equal rectangles. Then lay them out onto the baking tray, giving them each a bit of breathing space. Using the tip of a sharp knife, lightly score a border 5mm in from the edges of each rectangle, taking care not to cut all the way through.

Peel, core and slice the pear. Spoon the custard onto the pastry within the border, then lay the slices of pear on top. Brush the outer pastry border with a little milk. Then sprinkle with the ginger–sugar mix and bake for 10 minutes, or until the pastry is puffed up and golden.

Blueberry Mug Cake

I mean, really? A cake in a mug – surely this is too much to hope for? Nope it's not, it can be done, and even you and I can have one!

231 Calories | 6g Fat | 4.9g Saturates | 16.7g Sugars | 0.6g Salt

SERVES 1

30g self-raising flour

$1/_4$ teaspoon baking powder

$2^1/_2$ teaspoons caster sugar

3 tablespoons skimmed milk

$1/_2$ tablespoon coconut oil

$1/_4$ teaspoon vanilla extract

a handful of blueberries, plus

extra to serve (optional)

Combine all the ingredients, except the blueberries, in a large mug. Whisk until the batter is smooth, then stir in the blueberries – don't let them float on the top, stir them well in.

Cook in the microwave on high for about 1 minute – microwaves differ, so if the cake is not done, give it another 15-second blast. It'll be very hot, so hold back a bit before tucking in. If you like, you could sprinkle some extra blueberries on top.

Homemade Fruit Jellies

Jelly and ice cream anyone? Well, all you have to do is whip, wibble, wobble up and serve it with a single scoop of low-fat ice cream.

99 Calories | 0.2g Fat | Trace Saturates | 20.6g Sugars | 0.1g Salt

SERVES 4

4 gelatine leaves

600ml any flavour fruit
   juice (although pineapple,
   kiwi and papaya can make it
   difficult for the jelly to set)

2 tablespoons caster sugar

a handful of berries of your
   choice

Soak the gelatine leaves in a few tablespoons of fruit juice for about 5 minutes, or until they soften. Heat the remaining juice in a pan until hot. Stir in the sugar until dissolved. Drain the gelatine leaves, reserving the apple juice, then add them one by one and stir until dissolved. Add the reserved apple juice.

Divide the berries equally and place them in the bottom of four bowls. Pour in the jelly mixture. Transfer to the fridge – the jellies should take about 2 hours to set.

Tip

Next time you catch yourself heading to the fridge, ask yourself, is it really just because you're bored – find something to do instead, such as going for a walk.

Homemade Custard

Yes, of course we can have custard, are you mad!
It's safe, as I've used skimmed milk instead of
cream, and reduced the amount of sugar.

81 Calories | 1.5g Fat | 0.4g Saturates | 14.1g Sugars | 0.1g Salt

SERVES 4

150ml skimmed milk

1 teaspoon cornflour

50g caster sugar

1 medium egg yolk

$1/4$ teaspoon vanilla extract

Pour the milk into a small saucepan and slowly bring to a
simmer, then remove from the heat.

Put the cornflour, sugar and egg yolk into a bowl and whisk
together. Pour in the warm milk very slowly, whisking all the
time. Stir in the vanilla extract.

Strain the mixture back into the pan and heat again, very
gently, whisking all the time or the custard will start sticking
and burning. Once the custard just coats the back of a spoon,
remove from the heat and leave to cool completely before
pouring it over some homemade jelly (opposite) or serve
warm. It would also go very nicely with the Apple Pies with
Heart (page 154).

Lemon + Lime Sorbet

Yes, this has the demon sugar, but it's fat free and I'm a cup-is-half-full kinda gal!

63 Calories | 0g Fat | 0g Saturates | 15.2g Sugars | 0g Salt

SERVES 6–8

120g caster sugar

3 lemons (zest of 1 lemon and juice of all 3)

2 limes (zest of 1 lime and juice of 2)

1 medium egg white

berries of your choice, to serve

Pour 300ml cold water into a pan with the sugar and the zest of 1 lemon and zest of 1 lime. Put over a medium heat and keep stirring until the sugar dissolves. Then turn off the heat and leave to cool. Add the lemon and lime juice. Pour the mixture into a shallow container and put it in the freezer. Give it a stir every hour or so, otherwise crystals will form. When the sorbet is half frozen, beat the egg white into soft peaks and fold into the mixture. When the mixture looks as though it's beginning to set, freeze until it is firm. Serve with berries of your choice.

Tip

A little of what you fancy is always good, particularly when it's as healthy as this.

Greedy Girl's Chocolate Pudding

This recipe is for all you chocolate lovers. The dark cocoa powder gives it an intense chocolatey taste that's finished off perfectly with the crunchy nuts.

125 Calories | 7.5g Fat | 2.1g Saturates | 8.1g Sugars | 0.2g Salt

SERVES 4

2 bananas, peeled, sliced

then frozen

1 small avocado, peeled and

stoned

3 sticky pitted Medjool dates,

soaked in hot water for

15 minutes then drained

2 tablespoons good-quality

cocoa powder

2 teaspoons toasted chopped

hazelnuts

Put all the ingredients, apart from the hazelnuts, in a blender and blitz until smooth. Transfer to two small bowls, sprinkle the hazelnuts over the top and eat immediately.

Tip

Good news – studies have shown that chocolate is actually good for us. A small square of good-quality choc melted on the tongue 20 minutes before a meal triggers the hormones in the brain that say 'I'm full'!

Mini Victoria Sandwiches

Come on… surely it must be cake o'clock? This is a much healthier version of a traditional Victoria sandwich – I use half-calorie sugar and I've swapped butter for low-fat spread.

167 Calories | 7.8g Fat | 2.2g Saturates | 8.4g Sugars | 0.4g Salt

MAKES 12 CAKES/

SERVES 12

175g low-fat spread

90g half-calorie sugar

3 eggs

1 teaspoon vanilla extract

175g self-raising flour

a little icing sugar, for dusting

FOR THE FILLING

12 raspberries

6 teaspoons low-sugar raspberry
  jam

12 heaped teaspoons
  low-fat crème fraîche

Preheat the oven to 120°C/gas mark 1 and spray a 12-hole muffin tray with low-calorie spray. Cream together the low-fat spread and sugar in a large bowl until light and fluffy. Using an electric whisk, whisk in the eggs one at a time, then add the vanilla extract and mix in. Fold the flour into the cake batter and spoon the batter equally between the paper cases. Bake for 15–18 minutes until the cakes are well risen and golden brown. Remove the cakes from the tray and leave to cool on a wire rack.

While the cakes are cooling, make the filling. Mash the raspberries with a fork and swirl them into the jam and crème fraîche. When the cakes are cool, slice the top off each cake. Put a spoonful of filling on the bottom of each cake, slice the top in half and top the cake with these 'wings'. Dust with a little icing sugar.

Date + Apricot Balls

A little something sweet to have with your coffee…
but no more than two each, girls!

148 Calories | 8.8g Fat | 0.8g Saturates | 10.8g Sugars | Trace Salt

MAKES 16 BALLS/

SERVES 8

140g pitted Medjool dates

100g ground almonds

100g soft apricots

25g sesame seeds

Soak the dates in boiling water for 15 minutes, then drain.

Put them and all the other ingredients in a food processor and blitz until smooth. Then roll into 16 balls.

Keep in a Tupperware box for up to two weeks.

Skinny Soft Ice Cream

Now don't say I'm not good to you – I give you ice cream without the guilt as there's no sugar or cream in this recipe. Just don't be tempted to add sauce and a flake!

159 Calories | 3g Fat | 0.6g Saturates | 24.9g Sugars | Trace Salt

SERVES 4

4 large, very ripe bananas

2 tablespoons reduced-fat
   peanut butter

Peel and slice the bananas into 1cm thick discs, then lay them on a lined baking tray and put into the freezer until frozen.

Put the frozen bananas and peanut butter into a food processor and pulse/blitz. Keep going until the mixture is totally smooth and creamy. You can serve it now, or pop it back in the freezer if you want a firmer texture.

Tip

If the ice cream isn't creamy enough, you can add a couple of tablespoons of skimmed milk.

Apple Pies
with Heart

I've said it before and I will say it again and again: can the man, woman or child who invented 'light' puff pastry please be knighted by the Queen of England!

158 Calories | 4.3g Fat | 2.1g Saturates | 17.6g Sugars | Trace Salt

MAKES 4 PIES

100g ready-rolled light puff
   pastry

milk, for brushing

4 crispy dessert apples

2 tablespoons raisins

zest of $1/2$ lemon

1 teaspoon ground cinnamon

Preheat the oven according to the puff pastry packet instructions. Roll out the pastry and cut out four hearts about 7.5cm in diameter, using a heart-shaped cutter. Brush with milk, place on a non-stick baking tray and bake according to the packet instructions.

While the pastry is cooking, peel and core the apples and cut them into 2cm chunks. Put them in a saucepan with the raisins, lemon zest, cinnamon and 1 tablespoon of cold water. Cover and cook very gently for 4–8 minutes until the apples soften, keeping an eye on them and adding a few drops more water if they're drying out too much.

Pile the apples onto four plates and top with the puff-pastry hearts. You could also serve the baked apple with a little low-fat ice cream or custard instead of the pastry hearts.

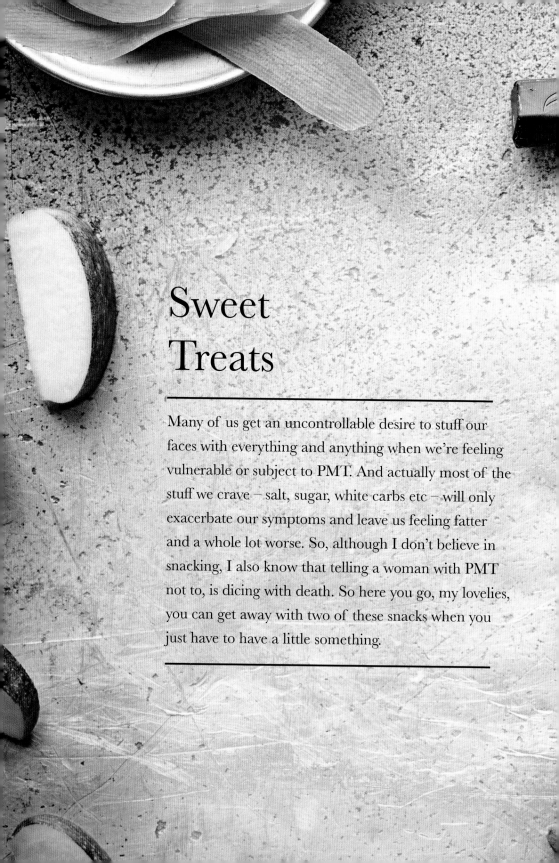

Sweet Treats

Many of us get an uncontrollable desire to stuff our faces with everything and anything when we're feeling vulnerable or subject to PMT. And actually most of the stuff we crave – salt, sugar, white carbs etc – will only exacerbate our symptoms and leave us feeling fatter and a whole lot worse. So, although I don't believe in snacking, I also know that telling a woman with PMT not to, is dicing with death. So here you go, my lovelies, you can get away with two of these snacks when you just have to have a little something.

4 squares of dark chocolate (about 70 per cent cocoa solids) with 4 almonds.

1 pitted Medjool date stuffed with 1 teaspoon of nut butter, such as almond, peanut or cashew.

200ml hot or cold skimmed milk with 2 teaspoons of chocolate syrup stirred in.

1 small apple, cored and filled with 1 teaspoon of brown sugar and 4 chopped hazelnuts, baked for 30–40 minutes at 180°C/gas mark 4 until tender.

½ small apple, sliced and spread with 2 teaspoons of nut butter, such as almond, peanut or cashew.

2 tablespoons pumpkin seeds spritzed with 1 teaspoon of vegetable oil and baked for 10 minutes at 180°C/gas mark 4.

2 kiwis.

1 small scoop of low-fat frozen yogurt in a small, plain cone.

1 carrot, cut into thin strips, dipped in 2 teaspoons of nut butter, such as almond, peanut or cashew.

1 green apple, sliced and spread with 2 teaspoons of almond butter.

Drinks

Beat
the Bloat

We all suffer the dreaded belly bloat at some time or another, and it can be so depressing, not to mention demotivating. There's nothing worse, if you've been eating healthily and exercising, than ending up looking six months pregnant anyway!

In fact, in the bad old days, whenever I got the belly bloat I would get so demotivated that I would self-medicate with slabs of cake – reeaaaally clever! But now, of course, I am far older and wiser (although I still use the cake method sometimes!) and I've learnt a few things along the way. For instance, I used to think that if I cut down on my fluid intake it would help the bloat, because there was less fluid to bloat up with. But that is most definitely not the case! And I know this because a genuine bona fide doctor told me, so there!

Get your drinking bottles out, girls, as water retention is our body's way of storing fluid so we don't dehydrate. So, in fact, if you have a bloating problem, you need to push the fluid out with more fluid, not restrict your intake. Fresh lemon juice has a diuretic effect and it also acts as a mild laxative if you drink it with warm water. So the first thing I do every morning after stumbling down the stairs, looking like I've been pulled through a hedge backwards, is to drink a pint of warm water and lemon. I then sip 1.5 litres mineral water throughout the day. Try it, girls, it will make a big difference.

Amazing Ginger + Cinnamon Tea

It's amazing because, although the sugar never comes near it, the cinnamon makes this drink beautifully sweet … and of course it's horribly good for you because it will settle that dicky tummy!

3 Calories | 0.1g Fat | 0g Saturates | 0.1g Sugars | 0g Salt

SERVES 1

2 x 6cm cinnamon sticks

1 heaped teaspoon grated
    fresh ginger

Put the ingredients in a saucepan with 300ml cold water and bring to the boil. Reduce the heat and simmer for 5 minutes. Remove from the heat and leave to steep for 10–15 minutes. You can leave it for hours and reheat, or drink half, add a bit more water and reheat… it's a very good-tempered tea.

Tip

Get your rest! A good night's sleep reduces levels of the stress hormone cortisol, which can make it more difficult to lose weight.

Vanilla Vodka

Now, obviously, if we don't drink any alcohol at all we lose weight faster, but I know that is completely unrealistic, so here are some skinny-girl cocktails. Measure with a proper pub measure as it so easy to glug-glug-glug hundreds of extra calories.

58 Calories | 0.2g Fat | 0.2g Saturates | 0.1g Sugars | 0g Salt

SERVES 1

ice cubes

1 shot of vodka

2 drops of vanilla extract

200ml sugar-free ginger ale

Fill a tumbler with ice cubes and pour the ingredients in. Give it a stir with your finger and sip – did you hear what I said there? – SIP.

Arriba, Arriba! Give me Tequila

This will get the party started but don't be tempted to have more than one or you could find yourself ordering a doner kebab by 'accident'.

52 Calories | 0g Fat | 0g Saturates | 0.1g Sugars | 0g Salt

SERVES 1

ice cubes

1 shot of tequila

200ml soda

a squeeze of lime

Fill a tumbler with ice cubes and pour the ingredients in. Mix well and serve.

V, L&S

In case you were wondering, a V, L&S is the 'cool' way to order a vodka, lime and soda.

56 Calories | 0g Fat | 0g Saturates | 0g Sugars | 0g Salt

SERVES 1

ice cubes

1 shot of vodka

200ml of zero Sprite

1 slice of lime

Fill a tumbler with ice cubes and pour the ingredients in. Mix well and serve.

Marvellous Mulled Wine

AHHH I just love the way this gorgeous mulled wine fills the whole house with the aroma of Christmas, as it bubbles away on the stove.

92 Calories | 0.2g Fat | 0.1g Saturates | 1.2g Sugars | 0g Salt

SERVES 12

1.5 litres good-quality red wine

zest of 1 orange

2 teaspoons ground cinnamon

$^1/_2$ tablespoon cloves

2 teaspoons ground ginger

1 teaspoon ground nutmeg

1 cinnamon stick

1 tablespoon clear honey

Pour the wine into a large saucepan over a low heat, then add the orange zest. Add the spices and let the wine simmer for 30 minutes. Stir in the honey, pour the wine through a strainer and serve in heatproof glasses.

Tip

Try not to drink too much of this – alcohol contains empty calories and more than half end up around your middle! Have just one unit every other day.

Mocktails

Raspberry Mint Spritzer

I have been known to have this rather lovely mocktail for an early morning breakfast.

18 Calories | 0.2g Fat | 0g Saturates | 1.8g Sugars | 0g Salt

SERVES 1

10 raspberries

10 fresh mint leaves,
   plus extra sprigs to serve

squeeze of lime

ice cubes

400ml low-calorie lemonade

Reserving two or three raspberries for decoration, put the raspberries and mint leaves into a highball glass, and, using a spoon or muddler, squish the juice from the raspberries. Then add the lime juice and some ice cubes before topping up with the lemonade. Top with extra sprigs of mint and the reserved raspberries.

Moscow Mule

This will kick you into the party mood!

5 Calories | 0.3g Fat | 0.2g Saturates | 0.2g Sugars | 0g Salt

SERVES 1

crushed ice

250ml low-calorie ginger beer

juice of $1/2$ lime

60ml soda water

Fill a short glass with crushed ice, then pour in the ingredients. Mix well and serve.

Blackberry Scramble

Try adding a single shot of vodka or gin.

37 Calories | 0.1g Fat | 0g Saturates | 7.5g Sugars | 0g Salt

SERVES 1

4–6 blackberries

450ml low-calorie lemonade

juice of $\frac{1}{2}$ lemon

2 teaspoons maple syrup

crushed ice

sprig of fresh basil, to decorate

Put the blackberries, lemonade, lemon juice and maple syrup in a cocktail shaker. Give it a good shake and pour over a glass of crushed ice. Decorate with a sprig of basil.

Banana Colada

You will need to plan for this one, as two of the ingredients need to be frozen.

130 Calories | 3.6g Fat | 3.1g Saturates | 19.6g Sugars | 0g Salt

SERVES 4

200ml light coconut milk

2 very ripe bananas, frozen

250g pineapple chunks in juice
   (drained of their juice)

250ml coconut water

Pour the coconut milk into an ice-cube tray and freeze overnight. You need to freeze the bananas and the pineapple chunks too. Then when you are ready for your mocktail, put all the ingredients into a blender and blitz until smooth. Pour into four glasses and you're ready to party.

Three-day Emergency Plan

Now, I want to make myself very clear here: you do not have to do this punishing three-day emergency/kick-start plan, but for a lot of people, it really motivates them to lose a lot of weight quickly at the beginning of their weight-loss. So if you want to shift some bloating fluid and fat and kick-start your system, or if you've only got a short time before you need to slip into your LBD, then dig deep and tap into that willpower. If you want, you could do the kick-start for a bit longer because it is healthy and well-balanced.

So my tips are as follows: drink a minimum of 1.5 litres water a day. Try to start every day with a mug of hot water with freshly squeezed lemon juice. Try not to deviate from the plan at all because if you are anything like me, you'll end up making swaps left, right and centre, and swapping white fish for white cake, and that won't get you anywhere… believe me, I've tried it.

	DAY 1	DAY 2	DAY 3
BREAKFAST	Skinny Eggs (page 173)	Super-skinny Breakfast (page 176)	Herby Omelette (page 181)
LUNCH	Skinny Bitch Soup (page 174)	Magic Weight-loss Soup (page 56)	Lemony Chicken (page 181)
DINNER	Skinny Bitch Sole + Greens (page 175)	Steamed Salmon + Greens (page 178)	Cod + Roasted Vegetables (page 182)

Skinny Eggs

Right this is it – we're off!
Come on willpower, we need you now!

53 Calories | 0.9g Fat | 0.1g Saturates | 0.7g Sugars | 0.5g Salt

SERVES 1

2 egg whites

1 teaspoon of your favourite
   dried herbs

freshly ground black pepper

a handful of spinach

Heat a non-stick frying pan over a medium heat and whisk together the egg whites, herbs and black pepper. Pour into the pan, and as it sizzles and starts to set, add the spinach. Keep the heat low and cover with a lid, for 2–3 minutes until the eggs are set.

Serve and eat slowly, savouring and chewing every mouthful, picturing yourself in that little black dress dancing your socks off, feeling like a million dollars.

Tip

It's a proven fact that, if we exercise, we live longer... in a slimmer body.

Skinny Bitch Soup

Yup, I know it's not much… but it's better than nothing, and soup has been proven to keep you full for longer! Keep yourself busy this afternoon so you don't think about food.

131 Calories | 2.6g Fat | 0.3g Saturates | 7.6g Sugars | 4.6g Salt

SERVES 1

500ml boiling water

20g sachet of miso soup

50g your favourite mushrooms,
   sliced

1 tablespoon dark
   or light soy sauce

1 teaspoon grated fresh ginger

50g shredded cabbage

50g beansprouts

2 spring onions, chopped

1 large courgette, spiralised
   or cut into thin strips

Put the water in a saucepan along with the contents of the miso soup sachet, the mushrooms, soy sauce and ginger. Add the cabbage, beansprouts and spring onions. Cook over a medium heat for 2 minutes, then put the courgette in a bowl and pour the soup over the top.

Skinny Bitch Sole + Greens

Drink lots of water before and after dinner and chew some sugar-free gum afterwards if you are wanting to nibble.

272 Calories | 7.8g Fat | 1.2g Saturates | 2.9g Sugars | 1.5g Salt

SERVES 1

1 x 200g fillet of lemon sole or any white fish

salt

200g tenderstem broccoli, cut into florets

1 teaspoon toasted sesame oil

a squeeze of lemon juice

Preheat the grill to a high heat, sprinkle a little salt on the fish and grill for 3–4 minutes, skin-side down, until the skin bubbles and blisters.

Steam the broccoli for a few minutes until just tender. Remove from the heat and drain, then drizzle the sesame oil on top and serve with the fish and a squeeze of lemon juice.

Tip

I'm a great believer in keeping a food diary. Don't just record what you've eaten, but when you've overeaten and how it made you feel.

Super-skinny Breakfast

I told you this wouldn't be easy.

134 Calories | 4g Fat | 0.9g Saturates | 0.6g Sugars | 1.7g Salt

SERVES 1

3 slices of skinless cold turkey

  or chicken

3 slices of cucumber

  or steamed asparagus

1 teaspoon pumpkin seeds

I have no other instructions other than make this last as long as possible. Think of the dress and the fat you could lose – over 2kg in these three days.

Magic Weight-loss Soup

Hang your dress up where you can see it to remind yourself that nothing tastes as good as being slim feels… kinda true!

131 Calories | 6.7g Fat | 0.9g Saturates | 4.5g Sugars | 1.4g Salt

SERVES 1

1 large bowl of Magic Weight-

  loss Soup (page 56)

1 teaspoon sunflower seeds

Spinkle the sunflower seeds over the top and enjoy.

Steamed Salmon + Greens

Only one more day of this super-strict plan to go and you will have lost pounds by the end of tomorrow!

250 Calories | 12.7g Fat | 2.1g Saturates | 4.1g Sugars | 2.6g Salt

SERVES 1

1 x 100g skinless salmon fillet

2 teaspoons dark or light soy sauce

2 spring onions, chopped

200g spinach

Put the salmon on a small, heatproof plate, drizzle the soy sauce over it and add the spring onions. Put the plate in the steamer and steam for 5–7 minutes. For the last couple of minutes, put the spinach in the top part of the steamer, then serve the salmon on top of the spinach and enjoy. If you are hit with hunger pains later in the evening, just have a large glass of water – trust me, it does stop the pain.

Tip

Salmon isn't only delicious, but will also make you happy – studies show it reduces the risk of depression.

Herby Omelette

I've used an egg, plus an egg white for extra protein, as protein is proven to keep you fuller for longer.

108 Calories | 7.3g Fat | 1.8g Saturates | 0.3g Sugars | 1.3g Salt

SERVES 1

1 egg, plus 1 egg white

1 tablespoon chopped
   flat-leaf parsley,

salt and freshly ground
   black pepper

½ teaspoon olive oil

Whisk the egg and the egg white together with the parsley and some seasoning, then heat the oil in a non-stick frying pan and fry the omelette until set to your liking.

DAY 3
Lunch

Lemony Chicken

Wait for this, girls, this is really good.

203 Calories | 7.4g Fat | 1.5g Saturates | 1.7g Sugars | 0.2g Salt

SERVES 1

100–120g skinless chicken breast

juice of ½ lemon

½ garlic clove, crushed

½ teaspoon olive oil

1 teaspoon sesame seeds

6–8 asparagus spears or any
   green veg you fancy

Put the chicken breast between two pieces of baking paper and bash it down flat with a rolling pin. Put it in a bowl, pour over the lemon juice, garlic and oil and rub into the chicken. Leave to marinate. When you are ready to eat, heat a griddle pan nice and hot and put the chicken on it for 3 minutes without moving it, then flip it over and cook the other side for a further 3 minutes.

Dry-fry the sesame seeds in a non-stick pan over a medium heat. Remove from the pan and set aside.

Steam or lightly boil the asparagus and serve with the chicken and toasted sesame seeds sprinkled over the top.

Cod + Roasted Vegetables

This is the last super-strict meal and then back on the gorgeous greedy girl's plan tomorrow!

299 Calories | 4.2g Fat | 0.7g Saturates | 9.3g Sugars | 1.4g Salt

SERVES 1

1 red pepper, deseeded
   and sliced

1 courgette, thickly sliced

1 red onion, sliced

light olive oil spray

salt and freshly ground
   black pepper

1 teaspoon dried oregano

1 x 250g skinless cod fillet

6 cherry tomatoes on the vine

zest and juice of ½ lemon

Preheat the oven to 200°C/gas mark 6. Put the red pepper, courgette and onion in a shallow baking tray and spray with the some oil. Season well with salt and black pepper and the oregano. Put the fish on top and spray with a little more oil. Lay the tomatoes on top of the vegetables, squeeze the lemon juice over the top, sprinkle over the lemon zest and bake for 10 minutes.

Tip

Mint is the perfect way to end your meal – but not covered in chocolate. Mint tea is known to aid digestion and relieve stress.

LBD-Day!

So tonight's the night when you and your LBD get to party the night away! You've worked your booty off (literally) and you are looking, and more importantly you're feeling, a million bucks! To make sure you feel top banana throughout the day, start your morning with a hot water and lemon to keep your digestive system working like a dream (and to leave you feeling saintly). It doesn't sound exciting, but you'll thank me, believe me.

Next, choose any of the breakfasts from the book but try to stay away from bread. Trust me! It's serious beat the bloat time today and wheat can bloat some people out in a dramatic way (it does me!)

Make sure you drink plenty of fluids all day and avoid salt. The last thing you need is water retention on your big night out! Now I know it sounds bizarre but it's a fact that the more water you give your body the less it will hold on to, so keep on sipping and ridding yourself of the bloat. Also being well hydrated will give you bags of energy for the dance floor as well as get you ahead of the game for any hangover you might get (a dry mouth is the second symptom of dehydration, the first is tiredness!)

Another great idea would be to treat yourself to a bit of a facial and a blow dry (you know you're worth it!) with all the money you must have saved by not buying chocolate, chips and wine for the last few weeks ...

You can of course give yourself a DIY facial at home instead. Here are two of my super easy foodie facial 'recipes':

Wet your face and then massage 1 tablespoon of baking soda into your skin (a brilliant exfoliator) in a circular motion then wash off with a facial cleanser. Or add a spoonful of sugar to any oil – olive, coconut (my favourite) or almond for example – and rub onto the skin in a circular motion and then rinse off.

Simply mix together 3 tablespoons of honey with 2 tablespoons of orange juice and 2 drops of neroli (orange blossom oil) and slather on your face. Then put a slice of cucumber or teabag that has been steeped and squeezed out on each eye and rest for 10–30 minutes.

This will leave your skin feeling fresh, glowing and primed for you to slap on the slap! There is an embarrassment of riches of step-by-step guides on how to make up your mush on YouTube, Pinterest and instagram. So why not make yourself a cuppa (minus a biscuit!) and take a little time out (again, you deserve it!) surfing the net to find exactly the look you fancy. I would also highly recommend you have a bit of a practice run before the party so as to avoid any disasters on the night. False eyelashes stuck to your chin will definitely ruin your 'look!'

The Little Black Dress

Now just a few words on underwear! Bet you weren't expecting me to come straight in with that one were you? But I must, as underwear can play a starring role in finishing off your LBD look. These days there are literally shelves upon shelves in every lingerie department in the land dedicated to displaying every kind of control underwear ever dreamed of. Yes, you can now, thanks to the wonders of modern (pants) science, de-wobble wobbly bottoms, flatten tummies, hold up (or down) large breasts, enlarge small ones, you can nip in waists, pad out bums and probably fly to the moon in a pair of top of the range tights if the fancy took you! Even skinnies use these super sleuth undercover agents as they are not just about holding lumps and bumps in, but are also about smoothing out your silhouette and giving you a great final look. So my advice is to go out a few days before the party and take your LBD with you so that you can make sure you are buying exactly the right piece for you and your uniquely wonderful bod!

Great tip alert! Make sure you try sitting down in the changing room to make sure you actually can. I've made the mistake of not taking the precaution of the 'sit test' before buying a suck-in-your-fat garment. Believe me it wasn't pretty! I paid the price of having to spend the entire night standing up rather than lying down.

When it comes to shoes, go as high as you can as this gives a longer, leaner look. Mind you if I'm honest mine usually end up in my bag with me dancing in my stockinged feet! Legs really can look slimmer with a pointy toed shoe (I know weird, right) and a 2-inch heel so avoid round-toed chunky heeled ones. If you are wearing nude tights, a nude shoe will make your legs look longer too. A trick used by our very own Duchess of Cambridge on a daily basis!

The Grub Bit

Now if there is going to be a dreaded buffet at the party consider having any of the dinners from that chapter before you leave. I don't know about you but buffet bars are a code red danger zone for me and for every overeater I've ever confided in. I get possessed by the food devil and will always find myself grabbing and grasping at anything and everything, even things I don't like! Deep-fried cockles anyone?!

But if you do decide that you are strong enough to indulge without over-indulging use the simple wonder of plate portioning for support. Simply visualise that your plate is divided into one half and two quarters. Then fill the half side with an abundance of colourful salad and veg, and then a quarter with meat or fish (not the battered prawns!) or egg and the second quarter with carbs, such as rice, potatoes or bread. But don't cheat (yes before you ask I have done it myself) by building an Everest-like pile of rice!

If you are planning on letting your hair down with a few drinks stay away from creamy cocktails. Prosecco, white wine spritzers or white spirits with diet mixers are the way forward as they are lower in calories. Vodka, fresh lime and soda is my favourite as it only has 50 calories and keeps me hydrated whilst getting tipsy at the same time. Bonus!

So you're wined and dined and have worked the room showing off how gorgeous you look, so all you have to do now is shimmy your way to the dance floor and dance the night (and the calories) away! Enjoy! You deserve it!

PS the Bacon Butty on page 37 is great for hangovers!

Index

Acknowledgements

I would like to say a huge thank you to:

My agent and friend, Melanie Blake, you are simply the best! *You only live twice!*

To Vicky Orchard, my editor, you have been brilliant. Thank you for realising my dreams with this book.

Maja Smend, the photos are absolutely stunning. Thank you, thank you, thank you.

Lizzie Harris, thank you so much for making all my recipes look so fabulous ... And for the great tequila!

Thank you Rachel Jukes, I want every single one of the props you bought for my house!

Nicky Collings, you have done an awesome job of designing the book ... Thank you for making me seem so classy!

Nicky Johnston... What can I say that I have not said a thousand times before? You are my favourite photographer. Simple as that.

Simone Volmer, thank you for my beauty – you keep it in your bag! You are not only a brilliant make-up artist, you are also a very dear friend …x

Fiona Parkhouse, I seriously don't think I could do a shoot without you! You know everything that needs to be known about clothes and you are a dear friend to boot! xx

And thank you to my darling husband and children … I love you with all my heart x

Leabharlanna Poiblí Chathair Bhaile Átha Cliath